Baseball in
EVANSVILLE

Baseball in EVANSVILLE

BOOMS, BUSTS AND ONE GLOBAL DISASTER

Kevin Wirthwein

THE
History
PRESS

Published by The History Press
Charleston, SC
www.historypress.com

Front cover, from left to right: author's collection; author's collection; Indiana Historical Society; author's collection; *bottom*: author's collection. *Back cover*: author's collection; *inset*: Tom Goelzhauser.

First published 2020

Manufactured in the United States

ISBN 9781467145589

Library of Congress Control Number: 2019954236

To my late parents, Alfred Francis Wirthwein and Virginia Mae Wirthwein.

And to Papa Bear, who showed me baseball.

CONTENTS

ACKNOWLEDGEMENTS

*H*istory books, I've learned, require skills beyond simply putting words onto pages. Most of those other skills I struggled to learn along the way. None of this would have been possible without the patience of some, the encouragement of many and the support of all.

First, to my mother, Virginia, who passed away while I was rounding third and heading home on this work. She never doubted and always loved and encouraged me. To my wife, Erin, for her patience and love, and to Lauren, Allison, Abby and Andrea, for the perspective that four unique daughters provide. The support of all family members was special. Like my mother, my siblings—David, Susan and Lisa—always assumed this book was a fait accompli when I doubted it myself.

My brother Chris, an author in his own right, is also a baseball memorabilia collector and historian. He'll never know how many offhanded author-like suggestions he made that I put into use. His love of baseball made no discussion of my topic a nuisance to him. Vince Waldron is another author who provided inspiration and validation through email exchanges. Vince is the author of *The Official* Dick Van Dyke Show *Book*. You'll have to read this book to understand the connection.

Special thanks to Willard Library archivist Patricia Sides for going out of her way to help me meet deadlines during the busiest week of her year. Jennifer Greene of the University of Southern Indiana provided invaluable assistance. Posthumous gratitude to George Spohr, late editor of the *Evansville Courier and Press*. George was incredibly responsive to my requests to use material from his paper. Indiana Historical Society, Evansville Vanderburgh Public Library and Bosse Field staff members amazed me with their warmth.

Thank you, friends and acquaintances, for cheering me from the beginning. Mark and Taylor Abell, Rick Wambach, Mark Senzell, Lois Unfried, John Moeller, Jeff Gabbard and Carol Schaefer all assisted in special ways.

INTRODUCTION

This book was to be about the Evansville White Sox, a Class-AA club that lasted all of three years, from 1966 to 1968. The "Esox" are my all-time favorite team. I didn't want to aim too high in my first book. Fifty years after watching them play in my first live game, I still had a lot to learn. I needed one brief chapter encapsulating the history of baseball in Evansville to open the book, then on to my beloved Esox. I thought a quick run through the Evansville baseball history books for material would be easy. What I found was disappointing. There were no Evansville baseball history books that started from the beginning. Most began around 1915, but I found that my hometown was playing baseball at least fifty years before that.

The people of Evansville have watched and played baseball since just after the Civil War. In 1877, the city entered a team into what is believed to be the first minor league. Despite high hopes, it failed. Keeping professional baseball in the river city was nearly impossible throughout the 1800s. Financial failures were the norm. Scandals and misappropriations were plenty. Colorful characters and weird events were everywhere. Teams came and went. When professional teams folded, the city filled its summers with semiprofessional and amateur ball. The history of Evansville baseball during the nineteenth century is extraordinary.

The twentieth century had its own unique influences, both good and bad. A couple of world wars and devastating floods interrupted the professional game. So did a pretty bad depression. Tragedies led to triumphs in some cases. An opportunistic mayor turned one tragedy into a historical first: the construction of the first municipally owned ballpark in the nation. Evansville mayors fought to keep professional baseball in Evansville. Most succeeded.

One future mayor loved baseball so much that he supported the city's first team in the Negro Southern League. That team consistently drew more spectators than did its white counterparts. Years without professional baseball were much like they were in the 1800s, filled with semipro excellence from both white and Negro teams. Wartime pitted leagues of factory and shipyard workers against each other. War also brought major-league spring training to Evansville.

Minor-league baseball exuberance peaked after World War II until the influences of entertainment and comfort technologies brought the system to its knees. Staying home to watch a game on television meant you could stay cool and grab a cold beer. At Evansville's stadium, beer was not allowed and air-conditioning not feasible. A crumbling ballpark was the death knell for the city's most stable franchise and its iconic manager. Then a super-salesman mayor resurrected professional baseball after eight long years of trying. A colorful local millionaire established Evansville as headquarters of a third major league, with disastrous results. The story of his attempt to challenge baseball's elites is most intriguing because of its enormity.

Evansville baseball history is filled with triumphs and tragedies, failures and comebacks, scandals and scoundrels, injuries and healing, heroes and heartwarming stories, movie stars and musicians, life and death.

As the story of the first one hundred years ended, another story of triumph began. It was all so interesting and sometimes romantic.

1

THE CIVIL WAR TO THE TWENTIETH CENTURY

1865–1900

The Beginning of Ball Clubs

Organized baseball was difficult to define in the latter third of the 1800s. Independent organized leagues formed as early as 1877. The Northwestern League signed the first agreement with the major leagues in 1882, called the "Tripartite Agreement." Structure was a long way off in the summer of 1865 as the nation embarked on recovery from a civil war and the assassination of a president. Baseball helped the healing.

Evansville's Crescent City Ball Club formed in 1865, as the war ended. Club members played choose-up and challenge games against all comers. Games were high-scoring and typically lasted four innings. Money usually changed hands. The Crescent City club had its own ball grounds. The *Evansville Daily Journal* followed games from around the country. Of a game between the National Club of Washington, D.C., and the Atlantics of New York, the paper pondered, "Hadn't the Evansville boys better challenge the victors for the championship?" The pride a city had in its hometown boys permeated the national landscape.

The newly established Evansville Ball Club met at the courthouse in May 1866 "to perfect its organization" and revise "rules and regulations" of baseball in Evansville. Many new clubs began to form. "The baseball epidemic is raging fearfully all over the country," wrote the *Daily Journal* in 1866. "While cities have it the worst, not a village, settlement or 'corners' has escaped the infection."

THE FIRST CHAMPIONSHIP OF EVANSVILLE

The Resolute Nine made news as a premier club as early as 1867. Players were compensated by putting up an agreed-to amount of money that game winners divided among themselves. Some players were paid under the table; some were openly compensated. Teams like the Cincinnati Redlegs had salaried players and some who received a share of gate receipts. In 1869, Cincinnati started paying salaries to all of its players, making it the first truly professional baseball team.

Called the Resolutes, the 1867 team invited a club from across the Ohio River in Owensboro, Kentucky, to visit for a summer game. A return game in Owensboro received great attention. The *Owensboro Monitor* noted that the Resolutes had been in existence for two years and were one of the oldest teams in the area. "Broken noses can be expected," said the *Monitor*. The Resolutes took the steamer *Ollie Sullivan* down the Ohio River to Owensboro for the game. Evansville fans were invited to follow for a round-trip fare of two dollars.

A *Journal* reporter wrote that Owensboro's uniforms were very similar to those of the Resolutes. Owensboro uniforms notwithstanding, the Resolutes prevailed, 59–21, before "a great crowd of spectators." Nary a nose was broken. A return match in Evansville was more competitive but again won by the Resolutes, 50–40. At each venue, the host team provided dinner, drinks and frivolity on evenings following play.

The high scoring was attributed to the "Knickerbocker Rules," laid down by William Wheaton and William Tucker of New York's Knickerbocker Baseball Club in 1845. Pitchers were required to "pitch" the ball underhanded, like a horseshoe. Pitchers developed speed and movement over time. Hurlers had some leeway in a "pitcher's box," a six-foot-square area in which they could move around. Batters could request a high or low pitch and were walked after six balls (changed to four in 1889). Fielders were bare-handed. Games were error-filled. Pitchers were not allowed to throw overhand until 1884.

The Evansville Base Ball Club played the Resolutes at least twice during 1867. On a July road trip, the EBBC routed Paducah, 60–47. The *Journal* proclaimed that the pair of September games between the Evansville clubs would decide the "Championship of the City." The EBBC lost both games, and the Resolutes were crowned undisputed champions.

Independent teams flourished in the tri-state area as the game gained popularity. In 1868, there were rumors that a local "colored" club challenged the EBBC to a match. Travel to other locales broadened during the early 1870s. The Evansville Base Ball Club played locally. It was complemented by a traveling team called the Riversides. The Riversides traveled to Indianapolis, New Albany and several small Illinois towns and began wearing handsome uniforms in 1871.

The 1872 Riversides extended road trips to Illinois, Iowa and Missouri. They stopped in St. Louis to play the Empires, a team that employed the services of a professional pitcher. The Riversides lost, 22–12. The longest trip of 1872, to New Orleans, was to play the Lone Star Club, purported to be the champions of the South. The Riversides won. The *Evansville Daily Courier* in 1875 wrote commentary on "the prevailing mania" and great interest in "the National Game." The mania was created by baseball.

The Evansville Eckfords accomplished feats that "astonished their friends and backers." The new club defeated the local Red Sox team at the Riverside grounds. The Red Sox, at the time, were considered champions of the city. The game was a good, old-fashioned thrashing, 31–13. When the Red Sox failed to meet the Eckfords for a return game within a "required" two-week period, the championship was awarded to the Eckfords. The *Daily Courier* reported that the Eckfords also claimed the championship of Indiana. The Eckfords continued their stellar play throughout 1876. In July, they traveled by the steamship *Bob Lee* across the Ohio River to Henderson, Kentucky, and triumphed, 24–21. Later, they rode the *Hotspur* to Owensboro to play the Eagles. The Eckfords won, 22–12, in front of "not less than 1,500 occupied seats."

The "Invincible Eckfords" met the Terre Haute Sycamores for an August game in Evansville and captured their "toughest game of the season," 16–14. The *Daily Courier* article contained a detailed inning-by-inning account of the game. The Eckfords were the sporting toast of Evansville. Clubs continued to sprout.

THE EVANSVILLE BLUES: LEAGUE BALL

Evansville joined the League Alliance with its first true professional team in 1877. The league was the first to include minor-league clubs. Proposed by Albert Goodwill Spalding, the league was a response to the threat of the International Association of Professional Base Ball Players. The International Association had been plucking players from rival

BASE BALL

THE EVENT OF THE SEASON.

Louisville vs. Evansville

THREE GREAT GAMES AT THE

Evansville Base Ball Park,

Thursday, Friday and Saturday,

May 24th, 25th and 26th.

These will be the first games ever played
by a

LEAGUE CLUB.

In this city, and, introducing as they do,

MANAGER CHAPMAN'S FAMOUS

Kentucky Giants,

Brilliant and Exciting Contests are Assured.

Price of Admission.........................50 cents
Children...25 "

Game to be called promptly at 4 o'clock.

ns. Tickets to be had at Warren's Music
Store, Bridwell's Drug Store, Miles' Cigar
Store. The Courier Office and at the Base
Ball Park. my23 4t

First League Alliance series for the Evansville Blues in 1877. *Author's collection.*

cities regardless of player contracts. The Alliance extended its powers to independent teams across the country, limiting the availability of players while protecting the sanctity of contracts. Evansville's entry was named the Blues.

The League Alliance was a mix of major- and minor-league members. Members played league and nonleague opponents. It also identified potential opponents that played by the same rules. The Alliance included teams from major cities like Cincinnati, Memphis, Milwaukee, Indianapolis, St. Paul and St. Louis among its twenty-eight members, many of whom played Evansville.

The *Evansville Daily Courier* provided extensive coverage of the Blues. A group of directors named the organization the Evansville Base Ball Club (EBBC). The EBBC attempted to secure itself financially by taking stockholders. One stockholder was Evansville's sitting mayor, John Jay Kleiner. Kleiner later served in the U.S. Congress for Indiana. Claude G. DeBruler, an attorney, was manager of the club. He was also editor, proprietor and part-owner of the *Daily Courier*, which explains the wonderful newspaper coverage.

Stock proceeds helped fund improvements to a ballpark near Crescent City Springs. Improvements included construction of an amphitheater and a ten-foot-high fence surrounding the field. The amphitheater accommodated up to five hundred people; more could stand. Crescent City Springs, later named Salt Wells Park and then Cook's Park, was located between Columbia and Maryland Streets on the near west side.

In May, the *Courier* announced that team managers had completed arrangements for their nine players. The roster had two locals and an assortment of players from Boston, Louisville, Nashville, Memphis and Chicago. The Blues' season opened at their refurbished field in late May, and the first home series was a doozy. The Blues welcomed National League charter member Louisville Grays for a three-game set on Thursday,

Friday and Saturday, May 24–26. The Grays, called the Kentucky Giants in Evansville papers, was a powerhouse club that would achieve a level of infamy in a game-throwing scandal before the season was over.

The opener attracted around three hundred fans in the amphitheater and a "large force" of spectators in the surrounding orchard and saplings. Many believed that club directors lost big revenue by not leasing the trees outside of the park. The Blues played well in the first game but lost, 9–7. Expectations rose slightly after a one-run Blues loss on Friday. The *Courier* called Saturday's game a "waxing." The Blues were slaughtered, 25–3.

The Blues faced other well-known teams, but attendance faltered. The National League's St. Louis Brown Stockings made a trip to the Lamasco-area ball field in early June. The Browns whipped the Blues, 9–2. The National League's Cincinnati Redlegs took a couple of games from Evansville in the Queen City in mid-June.

The First No-Hitter

Pitcher Thomas Simpson joined the club for manager DeBruler's offer of $175 per month after a trip to Cincinnati. The *Courier* noted, "He pitched the popular 'curved ball' so swiftly that no one was able to strike the balls." He previously pitched for both St. Paul and Memphis. Days after signing, the right-hander manned the Salt Wells Park pitcher's box during a 32–0 walloping of the Atlantics. Only two batters reached first base, both on errors. The performance was the first no-hit game in Evansville professional baseball.

Attendance surged when the Red Caps of St. Paul, Minnesota, visited, but the Blues lost, 9–0, on June 28. The *Daily Courier* said that stockholders still might make something of their investment. The Indianapolis Quicksteps traded home games with the Blues. They celebrated July 4 by whipping the Quicksteps in front of nearly one thousand people at their home park.

The Blues' most frequent opponent was the Memphis Red Stockings. The Red Stockings traveled to Evansville for games in May and June. After a Blues loss at home against Memphis on June 25, the visitors' *Daily Appeal* newspaper pointed out the problem. "Decisions of the umpire were manifestly prejudicial in favor of Memphis." The man umpiring was the Memphis manager. Opposing managers often officiated games as a means to ensure fairness.

A July doubleheader in Memphis attracted 1,200 spectators. Despite occasional large crowds, most games were witnessed by a handful of fans. The glow of the first league experience diminished rapidly by midsummer, as it did for many of the League Alliance members. A July 19 *Courier* headline read, "The Evansville Blues a Thing of the Past." The team disbanded, and players were paid off. Memphis had disbanded two days earlier. Philadelphia followed a week later.

The Blues' troubles continued after the team's demise. "Courts are unhappy reminders of failure, and inexorably revive the ghosts of transactions long since dead," wrote the *Courier*. The club was sued for $875 for nonpayment of construction costs of its ballpark's fence and amphitheater. Evansville, Cairo and Memphis Company railroad filed suit for $55 owed for unpaid fares to and from Memphis. The first professional baseball club started with hope and ended in a pile of debt.

SEARCHING FOR A LEAGUE

After the League Alliance experiment, Evansville fielded teams that fit the semiprofessional definition. The Evansville Haymakers played teams from Indiana and adjoining states during 1879. The Haymakers became the Evansville Browns in 1880 and collected players from the Riversides, a club formed years earlier. The Browns played at Bedford and Salt Wells Parks and were recognized as the best "amateur nine" in the state of Indiana, according to the *Courier*.

The Riversides came back on the scene in 1883. The *Courier* often reported how much the players split from gate receipts for specific games. At midseason, the Riversides began making improvements to Salt Wells Park, the old Blues field. Work commenced on a nine-foot fence around the diamond with plans to build a large amphitheater seating 2,500 people. The amphitheater was modeled after a ballpark in Cincinnati. Construction began in late June, and the Riversides played one of their first games at the refurbished field on July 31 against the Excelsiors of Vincennes. The field was renamed Riverside Park.

BIG SAM AND THE NORTHWESTERN LEAGUE

Evansville's second professional league affiliation was in 1884. The city was first denied admission to the Northwestern League. Undaunted, the Evansville team played Northwestern League teams until July 26, when it replaced Terre Haute's exiting club. Terre Haute was so far behind on payment of their $4,000 league entry fee that it tossed in the towel. League managers decided that Evansville could join but was permitted to play only exhibition games with no chance at the championship. Locals wondered what Evansville gained by joining. The *Spalding Guide* shows Evansville won twenty-seven games and lost nine against Northwestern League teams. The record was far better than any of the other eleven teams.

The most notable historical player surfaced in 1884, when Sam Thompson, from Danville, Indiana, signed with the Evansville club. An Evansville scout had trekked to Danville and found "Big Sam" working on a roof in nearby Stilesville. When asked to play ball, Thompson was reluctant to give up his carpentry career and travel 150 miles to Evansville, but he agreed. The league folded in early August, and Sam played just a few games. Sam Thompson entered the Baseball Hall of Fame in 1974 via voting by the Veterans Committee. His lifetime major-league batting average was .331 in fifteen seasons. He still holds the record for ratio of runs-batted-in to games played. A plaque commemorating Thompson is located outside of Danville, Indiana.

One of the club's big wins came in late April against a city team that became a constant rival: Terre Haute. The Evansvilles knocked off the Hottentots, 4–0, at Salt Wells Park. The team looked good, sporting "Evansville" across the chest of their light-blue uniforms with dark blue trim and stockings. Terre Haute rooters complained loudly throughout the game about the umpiring of Hugh Dunlevy, a former player with the Evansville Browns. Evansville traveled to Terre Haute and won, 17–13, in front of 1,200 fans.

YEARS OF HOPE

Baseball in Evansville continued without a professional league affiliation. Hugh Dunlevy organized a strong team in 1885. Hope was high for a league team in 1886 as players from the 1884 team often visited Evansville. Their visits sparked rumors that they would again form a team in Evansville. Competitive teams visited and played in Evansville against solidly assembled local clubs in 1886. The F.W. Cooks team faced Nashville in an August game at Salt Wells Park that drew 1,200 fans.

In early 1887, F.W. Cook was putting together the new Ohio Valley League, which would include area teams, including Terre Haute and Henderson (Kentucky). With Dunlevy as manager, a professional team seemed like a sure thing. Cook said he would provide uniforms of old gold, blue stockings and a belt. The new duds would have blue letters across the chest spelling the club's name. Sadly, the Ohio Valley League never organized.

THE CENTRAL INTER-STATE LEAGUE AND A NEW BALLPARK

At the St. George Hotel in January 1889, a new Baseball Association agreed to sell capital stock worth $5,000 to join the Central Inter-State League. The association directors decided that they needed a first-class place to play and agreed to construct a new ballpark.

They eyed a parcel of land on Louisiana Street between Baker and Read Streets adjacent to, and owned by, the Union Stockyards. Enthusiastic stockyard representatives accepted a proposal for use of the plot from the Baseball Association. The owners figured it was worth $300 per year—$200 for the land plus $100 for taxes. The stockyard kicked in $250 and gave the Baseball Association $200 of existing fencing. By late February, plans were drawn up and work began on a field with wood grandstands seating 2,500.

The new field was referred to as League Park. It was used for other civic and sporting events, but its main purpose was for baseball. Adjacent to the playing field were the Union Stockyards Hotel on Baker Street and a beer garden. The Evansville Street Railway Authority put in new tracks to the grounds. Work on the grandstand amphitheater progressed by the middle of March. The playing ground was plowed and leveled by Arthur Saunders, a civil engineer and a former ballplayer.

League Park opened on April 7, 1889, with an exhibition-game victory over a St. Louis team called the Prickly Ash Bitters. Upwards of two thousand tickets were sold at the gate. Evansville's team was nicknamed the Hoosiers. The president of the ball club was F.W. Cook, who operated a well-known brewing company. Ed Pabst, out of St.

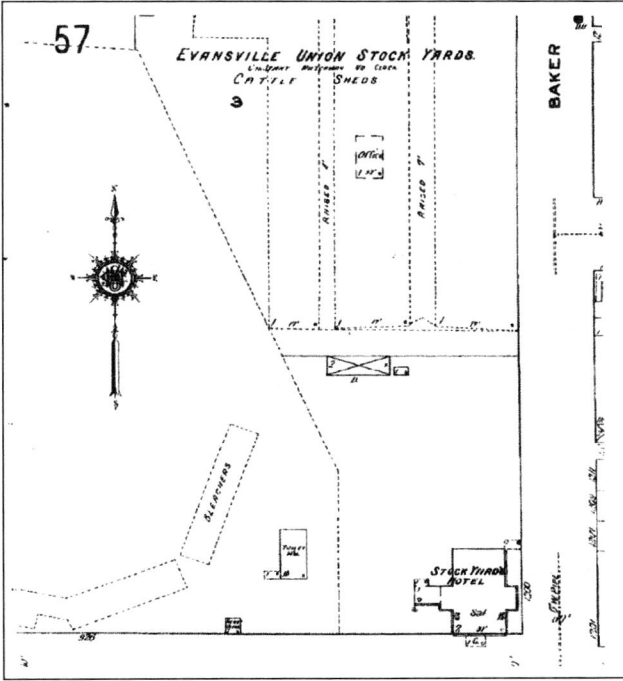

Left: Built in 1889, the Louisiana Street ballpark was next to the Union Stockyard Hotel. *Courtesy of Willard Library Archives.*

Below: A horse shed, beer garden and bowling alley were adjacent to League Park. *Courtesy of Willard Library Archives.*

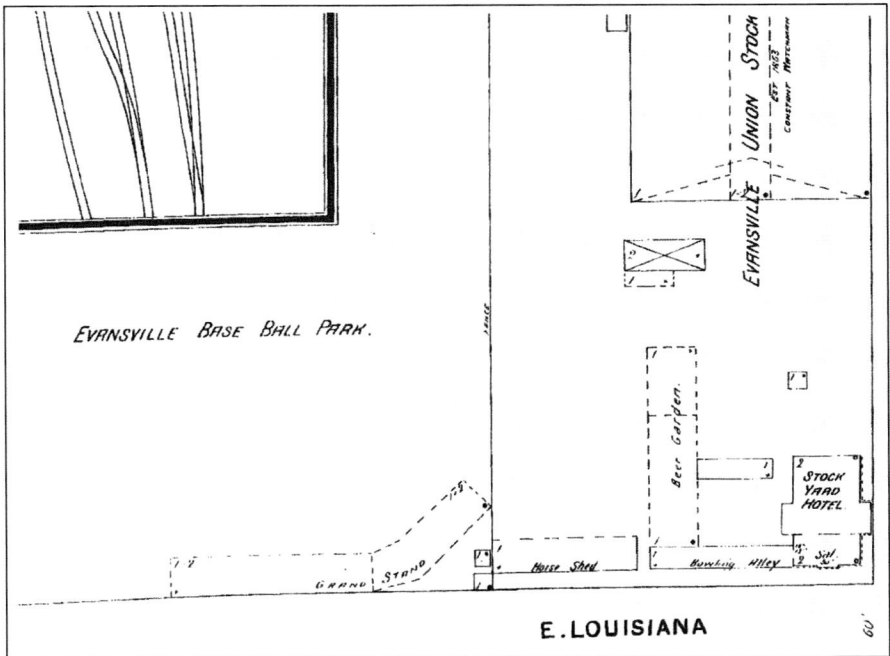

Louis, was an opponent on the Prickly Ash Bitters team for the opening of League Park and stayed to play for Evansville. Hoosier first baseman Lewis Whistler appeared in a league-leading 116 games and paced the Central Inter-State with 22 homers.

The Central Inter-State League hung together for the entire season. Evansville finished in the cellar with a record of 52-61. One of its most colorful and nationally reported-on players was a very young pitcher.

"WEE" WILLIE MCGILL: THE NO-HIT KID

Many baseball historians have written about fifteen-year-old Willie McGill of the 1889 Evansville Hoosiers. Willie pitched a 3–0 no-hitter at the Louisiana Street Park against the Davenport Hawkeyes on July 26, 1889.

"The game yesterday was probably as fine a display as will ever again be witnessed on the home grounds," began the *Courier* story the next day. The story included an inning-by-inning account of the contest. Despite four Hoosier errors, three bases on balls and one hit batsman, the fuzzy-faced teenager held Davenport without a hit or a run. The last out came when the visiting batter popped out to the Evansville shortstop. The pitching gem took just ninety-five minutes to play. Davenport's *Daily Times* listed the youngster at just five feet, three inches tall and 133 pounds.

The *Buffalo Express* said this about the young Evansville hurler: "He's like a little girl's definition of a sugar plum, round and rosy and sweet all over, and he throws barrel hoops and corkscrews at the plate."

Many papers cited McGill as the youngest player in pro ball. The hazards of using young players were exemplified by McGill, whose erratic conduct developed into a "drinking and carousing" problem. The influence of older players took its toll. The *Courier* wrote story after story about the team's debauchery and boozing on nights before games. The paper made frequent pleas to the club directors that

"Wee" Willie McGill, pitcher for the Evansville Hoosiers. *Indiana Historical Society, P0413.*

players retire by 10:00 p.m. Local scribes sprinkled in late-season accusations of play being influenced by gamblers. A month after his no-hitter, the Hoosiers cut Willie loose.

The next year, Willie stuck with Cleveland of the Players League, a major league at the time. Cleveland's team was owned by Charles Comiskey, later the owner of the Chicago White Sox. McGill was a phenom in his first major-league season. He is the youngest major-leaguer to toss a complete game and hurl a shutout. Both feats came while he was sixteen years old. At seventeen, he was the youngest major-leaguer to win twenty games in a season.

Willie made it back to Evansville to pitch four games for the Evansville River Rats in 1902, winning one game and losing one. The McGill victory stopped a fourteen-game Terre Haute winning streak in front of a September crowd of four hundred at League Park. He struck out six Terre Haute Hottentots. Willie was an old twenty-eight by this time.

McGill continued pitching semiprofessionally into his forties as his career turned to coaching and athletic training. He served short stints as baseball coach at both Northwestern University in Chicago and Butler University in Indianapolis, where he was athletic trainer for many years. He was the trainer on legendary Butler coach Tony Hinkle's 1929 national championship basketball team. McGill coached Butler's baseball team in 1929 and 1932.

SCANDAL: HARRINGTON THE HORRIBLE

Evansville returned to the Central Inter-State League in 1890, but the circuit fell to pieces in August. "With the whole business wrecked, the Evansville management duped, the boys left in the soup and all are mourning for Willie Harrington who skipped town yesterday morning and is supposed to have in his possession the boodle." The *Courier* was explaining that the Evansville manager left town with what little money the team had.

Harrington was blamed for the league's demise. He wasn't liked by his own players, who constantly disputed his leadership. The circuit started with six teams: Evansville, Burlington, Terre Haute, Peoria, Quincy and Galesburg (Illinois). Indianapolis took over the Galesburg franchise before the end of May and ran it into the ground before quitting on July 9. The Hoosiers led the league at 39-18 when Indianapolis exited. Down to five teams, directors decided to start over. New schedules were issued, and all remaining teams restarted with 0-0 marks.

Terre Haute dropped out on August 10. With four teams left, clubs made their own scheduling plans. Harrington had agreed to play six games at Burlington but packed up his team and departed after only three. Evansville Baseball Association president George Viehe met with Harrington at League Park on August 17 to "straighten things out." The next morning, Viehe was informed that Harrington had left Evansville on the evening train, taking ninety-five dollars from an overdrawn salary account. There were charges that Harrington sold players and never accounted for the money. Evansville had to withdraw from the league. The remaining clubs closed shop. Harrington was never heard from again.

Third-place Quincy was presented the Reach Trophy as the league winner for 1890 after the top two teams—Terre Haute and Evansville—dropped out. Evansville and its league troubles weren't unique in the profession. Of fourteen minor leagues that started in the spring of 1890, only seven survived the season.

A RETURN TO THE NORTHWESTERN LEAGUE AND MORE TURMOIL

Evansville was admitted to the Northwestern League in 1891 with Detroit, Dayton, Bay City (Michigan), Grand Rapids, Peoria, Fort Wayne and Toledo. Evansville players wore cadet gray flannel with the city's name across the front in maroon, the same color as their stockings. Caps were gray with maroon trimmings.

The Hoosiers started with April exhibition games against National League Cincinnati at League Park. The Reds won the first game but fell in game two. "My, oh! My! How the [Evansville] boys did bat the gilt-edged twirlers of [Cincinnati manager] Loftus' aggregation," wrote a special correspondent to the *Sporting News*. In May, the Hoosiers won two from league opponent Detroit in League Park. A Sunday crowd of nearly 1,800 saw a Hoosier win. Detroit won the Monday contest that was shortened to six innings so that its players could catch a train.

Bay City was in town for a Friday game and lost, blaming shoddy umpiring. The visitors won on Saturday. The Bay City win so enraged the Evansville crowd that "a shower of rocks and brick bats" were thrown on the field. Bay

City players accused the Hoosiers of sharpening their spikes before games. Two Bay City players were so badly spiked that they couldn't play at Peoria. One of the two was taken to a doctor. Bay City officials said they would never play in Evansville again.

Bay City and Detroit dropped out of the league in June. The Northwestern League reorganized into a six-team circuit. With Peoria holding down first place and Evansville in third, the league office declared "all games played so far are off, and the race begins now." The Hoosiers changed to black shirts, pants and stockings, white belts and black-and-white-striped hats for the restart. The new duds were wasted. Dayton withdrew, and Peoria defaulted on a payment guarantee to the league in July. Evansville was in fourth place after evenly splitting thirty-two games. Only Evansville, Grand Rapids, Fort Wayne and Terre Haute remained, but they gave it a go. The last Michigan team packed it in on July 30.

The Northwestern League was dead by mid-August. Fort Wayne was the only club that remained. It played exhibition games under the league banner until baseball season ended. *Spalding's Official Baseball Guide* shows that Evansville led the league with eleven wins in twelve tries when it came to an end.

THE I-I LEAGUE: ANOTHER FAILURE

Evansville joined teams from Illinois and Iowa to form the I-I League in 1892. The geographically dispersed Illinois-Iowa circuit fell apart. Quincy disbanded in late June. Aurora (Illinois), a club that had recently replaced Peoria, dropped out two days into July. The remaining teams from Aurora, Joliet, Evansville, Rockford, Terre Haute, Jacksonville and Rock Island played on in "a second season," until Aurora left on July 1. A week later, the Hoosiers departed the I-I because June "patronage at the games was miserable." The club was in third place. The Illinois-Iowa League was defunct by August.

Playing continued without a true professional team for the next couple of years. The 1894 "Champions of Evansville" baseball were crowned in October when 1,500 people witnessed the Buckskin Breeches defeat the F.W. Cooks at League Park. The Buckskin Breeches featured a battery of Fred Ossenberg on the hill and Julius Knoll behind the plate. Both were destined for the professional game. The *Journal* reported that Evansville had a chance to join one of two leagues through a reorganization of the old Inter-State and Northwestern Leagues, but the Southern League was the destination for the Pocket City.

BLACKBIRDS SCANDAL, 1895

Two gentlemen, Ollie Beard and William Stallings, drove the Southern League selection. Beard, who played for Evansville in 1884, was named field manager and served as an able shortstop. Stallings took the role as business manager. They put up $500 of the league's required $1,000 guarantee in January. The Evansville Blackbirds wore solid black uniforms with a white "E" on the front. Following a parade and an address by Mayor Anthony C. "AC" Hawkins, a crowd of around two thousand witnessed Evansville demolish Nashville, 17–6, on Opening Day. Beard slugged one of three Blackbird home runs.

The Blackbirds led league standings for most of the season, but patronage dropped as the schedule wore on. On June 26, the *Atlanta Constitution* reported that Evansville was no longer a member of the Southern League. The paper said that Evansville's franchise had been sold to Mobile and players were being transferred to that city, where "the fight for the pennant will go on." The *Constitution* jumped the gun. Instead of shuffling off to Mobile, the franchise was voted over to the Evansville Baseball Association and obtained financial backing from the Cook Brewing Corporation. The exuberance lasted a month before money troubles resumed, and the *Evansville Courier* began reporting that the Blackbirds had agreed to "throw games." They were in first place at the time. An August 21 *Courier* headline read "Looks Much Like a Deal."

The *Courier* said that Evansville's management team consented to "pass" games to Atlanta. Curious was the fact that the next series, due to be played in Evansville, was inexplicably moved to Atlanta. The change in quality of play became evident to fans and baseball writers. Evansville pitchers complained about lack of support. The rumor mills said management agreed to allow Atlanta to win the pennant for $1,500. The Blackbirds were to win just enough games against other Southern League teams to give the Atlanta Crackers a safe lead.

Money matters were so bad that local businessman and baseball enthusiast Gabe Simons had recently paid the Blackbirds' railroad fare out of town. On August 28, the *Nashville Tennessean* received word that Evansville players were not getting their full salaries. Pitchers Ernie Mason and Dan McFarlan

OLLIE BEARD,
Who Hopes to Defeat Nashville To-Day.

Ollie Beard, manager of the 1895 Evansville Blackbirds. *Author's collection.*

had jumped the club on the twenty-seventh. Second baseman Sam Mills followed. There were rumblings that Evansville would not show up for a scheduled series in Nashville. Netler Worthington, secretary of the Evansville Baseball Association, put the rumor to rest. He sent a telegram to Nashville manager George Stallings: "We are poor, but honest, and will certainly fill our engagement at Nashville. We think our share of receipts will greatly help us out."

The season played out as predicted by the *Courier*. On the final day of the season, a depleted Evansville roster lost two games to the Nashville Seraphs and finished third. Atlanta and Nashville ended in a virtual tie, but Nashville led by percentage points: .670 to .667. The *Courier* clarified years later that Evansville "sold" a total of six games to Atlanta. The sellout didn't go as planned for the Atlanta Crackers. The idea of a three-game playoff was proffered by league directors to break the tie. Atlanta declined the invitation to play Nashville.

At a September league meeting in Chattanooga, Nashville was voted the pennant. In late September, league president J.B. Nicklin canceled the vote because most league teams were not represented in Chattanooga. Montgomery sent a proxy that carried "iron-clad" instructions to vote against Atlanta, while Evansville held Atlanta up for an alleged $134.45 debt owed them in consideration of their vote. The debt was for games Evansville won for which Atlanta did not pay its guarantee.

The Evansville Baseball Association sent a stockholder to collect. Failing to secure a promise of payment from Atlanta, Evansville transferred its proxy to Nashville. Atlanta and New Orleans didn't show for the vote. Nicklin ruled that the two teams would remain tied until the Southern League's next meeting in December, hoping to get a quorum. The meeting, in Birmingham, had a quorum. *Sporting Life* reported that, after much discussion, the directors, or their proxies, endorsed the results of the September meetings. It was Nashville. "Atlanta kicked to the last, but was not upheld in the kick," reported *Sporting Life*'s correspondent.

The Blackbirds were not invited back to the Southern League for the 1896 season.

HEAVY HITTERS, 1895

The scandalous Blackbirds finished with sixty-six wins and thirty-eight losses. At least a dozen players on the team either had played or would play in the major leagues. They scored at a prolific rate. Center-fielder Claude McFarland led the league with a robust total of 149 runs scored in seventy-seven games.

Manager Beard signed local pitcher Fred Ossenberg in late March. Ossenberg drew accolades from many sources. The editor of *Sporting Life* wrote that Ossenberg would "climb to the top of the ladder" with a little encouragement and support. Ossenberg delivered, winning ten games and losing four. He played organized ball for another couple of years but never reached the big leagues.

Another Evansville boy, nineteen-year-old Charlie Dexter, played infield and outfield. Dexter was back after studying two years at the University of the South in Sewanee. Dexter took a job as society and drama editor of a local newspaper, the *Evansville Blotting Pad*, and played ball. He batted a respectable .288 and missed the controversial end of the season with a broken finger. Dexter and retired baseball friend Frank Houseman were recognized as heroes in 1903, when they broke open exit doors and ushered as many as 300 patrons out of the burning Iroquois Theater in Chicago before fleeing themselves. More than 1,700 people were in the theater, and 605 died on that December day, making it the deadliest single-building fire in U.S. history.

Dexter spent eight years in the major leagues with the National League's Chicago, Louisville and Boston clubs. Charlie Dexter continued in the minors until after the 1908 season. He spent his later years writing baseball articles. In 1934, Charlie committed suicide by gunshot in Cedar Rapids for unknown reasons.

Most astounding was a single-game hitting display put on by right-fielder Hercules Burnett on May 28. He slammed four home runs out of League Park in a 25–10 win over the Memphis Giants. Burnett needed all four long balls to top Ollie Beard, who knocked out three home runs. Burnett slugged twenty-six long balls on the season. Beard led the club in hitting at .376. Burnett came in at .349 and was third in the league with 110 runs scored.

League Roulette:
Kentucky-Indiana and Central

The Kentucky-Indiana League formed in 1896. Evansville's K-I entry included several players from the 1895 Southern League team. Brothers Ed and Fred Ossenberg played first base and pitched, respectively, before moving to the Madisonville (Kentucky) team midway through the season. Ed went into law enforcement after baseball and became chief of detectives of the Evansville Police Department. Fred was Vanderburgh County Republican chairman for many years.

The team included young center-fielder Harry Stahlhefer and pitcher and manager Adolph Stahlman. Stahlman was a juvenile probation officer after baseball and discovered future Hall-of-Famer Chuck Klein playing on the sandlots of Indianapolis in 1927. The K-I quickly evaporated. Vincennes (Indiana) exited at the end of June. Madisonville left as July came to an end. Henderson was gone a week later. Teams from Owensboro, Hopkinsville, Washington and Evansville retained their players and gave exhibitions for the remainder of the season.

The new Central League was organized in 1897 by prominent business leader Gabe Simons, who was appointed president. He was the same man who had paid railroad fares for the Blackbirds a couple of years earlier. Evansville, Terre Haute, Nashville, Cairo, Washington and Paducah were the clubs competing for the CL pennant as a Class-C circuit. The home team was called the Evansville Brewers. Hoping to improve on past league failures, Simons attempted to introduce order by setting a salary limit and required an up-front fee of $300 from teams as a show of fiduciary seriousness.

King for a Day

One early Brewers signee was left-handed pitcher Linwood Clifton Bailey, nicknamed "King." Bailey had kicked around professional baseball since 1891, mostly in the Southern Association. He made it to the big leagues for one winning game with Cincinnati in 1895 but shuffled back to the Southern Association after that. Bailey signed as Evansville's highest-paid player when he thought the Southern Association was out of business. Bailey wasn't fond of cold weather and complained his arm wouldn't loosen up until the weather got warmer. He had moderate success until the first Sunday in June, during a road game against the Paducah Little Colonels.

"The game was the finest ever witnessed," touted the *Courier*. King Bailey set down the Little Colonels one after another in a 1–0 no-hit shutout. Almost matching Bailey's perfection that day was Paducah southpaw Pete Dowling, who allowed only one.

King Bailey's no-hitter wasn't enough for the club to swallow his high price. He was labeled a "sore disappointment" and was released from the club in June with a record of eight wins and six losses. He pitched in the Southern Association through the 1903 season and found his calling as baseball coach at Mercer University. After coaching, Bailey found success in the insurance business.

SIMONS'S FOLLY

Gabe Simons's attempt to restructure the league failed. There were no means to enforce salary limits or any of Simons's rules. By the end of July, the league was in disarray. Simons resigned as president amid accusations that he was partial to Evansville by assigning sympathetic umpires to Brewers games.

After Simons's resignation, Evansville refused to play the third game of a series at Henderson. The Henderson manager paid Evansville its forty-dollar guarantee for the first game of the series but was nowhere to be found after the second game. Instead, he took a boat across the Ohio River to visit Simons and Evansville manager Julius "Hub" Knoll to find out if Evansville would be in business after the trip.

On July 21, the *Courier* declared the Central League "a thing of the past," with Evansville sitting in first place with forty wins and twenty-nine losses. Two days later, the *Courier* detailed a fight in front of the Wellington Hotel in Evansville. The skirmish between two Brewers players started when pitcher John Grimes accused second baseman Jack Corbett of saying that Grimes was "worse than Gabe Simons." Simons's new reputation made the accusation fighting words.

In August, the league sued Simons for $525. The sum included alleged overcharging of teams for his salary and failure to collect Nashville's entry fee. Besides Simons's inept leadership, a part of the league's problem was that salary rules were ignored by even the most threadbare towns. The

Washington (Indiana) club paid players way beyond the town's means. Attendance for Washington home games ranged between five and fifty spectators, and not all were paying customers.

THE KNOLLS

Evansville-born player-manager Hub Knoll was twenty-one years old when the city's Central League club fell apart. He had a younger brother, nicknamed "Punch," who grew up to be a baseball legend in Evansville. Hub's prowess as a player diminished after he was accidentally shot in the eye by older brother Punch during an 1896 hunting trip. He continued as a minor-league player and then turned his focus to managing. Julius "Hub" Knoll managed several teams throughout the minor leagues until the end of the 1905 baseball season.

Hub Knoll's career as a manager was on the rise after leading the 1905 Dayton team in the Central League. Sadly, in February 1906, Hub contracted typhoid fever. He suffered with the disease for five weeks in a Columbus, Ohio hospital and died just three hours before his mother, Laura, arrived from Evansville to visit. When Laura Knoll learned that her son was gravely ill, she hastened to Columbus, hoping to see him one last time. Julius Knoll, named after his father, was thirty years old when he died on March 23, 1906. He was transported back home to Evansville for burial.

2

RIVER RATS, YANKEES, EVAS AND WAR

1901–18

The Original Three-I League

Evansville was eager for another try at professional baseball when it joined the Three-I League—the Indiana-Illinois-Iowa League—as the River Rats in 1901. Evansville raised the $250 necessary to join the new league, along with teams from Terre Haute (Indiana), Bloomington (Illinois), Cedar Rapids (Iowa), Rockford (Illinois), Davenport (Iowa), Rock Island (Illinois) and Decatur (Illinois), for a 112-game schedule. Rock Island native Michael Sexton was named president. Sexton became a significant figure in solidifying the future of minor-league baseball.

Scribes referred to the circuit by other names, such as the Three-Eye League, or sometimes the Tri-Orb League, to add variety to their stories. *Sporting Life*, the preeminent sports publication of the era, referred to it as the "Three-Eyed League." Homegrown outfielder Punch Knoll was the first River Rat to bat in the first game of the new beginning in professional baseball.

Home Run Champion of the World

Evansville catcher Frank Roth knocked thirty-six fair balls out of Three-I League parks in 1901. Roth stroked two home runs off future Baseball

ROTH PROBABLY CHAMPION HOME RUN HITTER OF WORLD

FRANK ROTH.

Boy Who Wears the Mask for Evansville Has Gotten Thirty-three Homers During Season — His History

Catcher Frank "Germany" Roth set a world record in 1901 for the River Rats. Evansville Courier.

Hall of Fame pitcher Mordecai "Three-Fingered" Brown in a game at League Park that set a city attendance record. Brown threw for the eventual league champion Terre Haute Hottentots in front of more than 2,600 fans.

That wasn't Roth's only multiple home run game of the season. In mid-May, he knocked two out of League Park against Davenport. The *Courier* said the first long ball went over the fence. In the ninth inning, Roth "drove the ball into a hole under the left field fence and got a home run" with the bases full. Evansville lost, 13–9.

"Roth Probably Champion Home Run Hitter of [the] World" read a *Courier* headline after he slugged his thirty-third long ball. The homer surpassed "Buck" Freeman's 1899 season total as a player with the Brooklyn National League club, according to the paper. There is evidence to dispute the claim, but in the eyes of the *Courier* sports reporter and all available research, he was the champ. Roth added to his "record" with his thirty-sixth long ball on the last day of the season. Research done more than seventy years later disputed Roth's home run count as something less than three dozen, but the story of 1901 was Home Run Roth. He finished with a .323 batting average.

Nicknamed "Germany," Roth was five feet, seven inches tall and weighed 165 pounds. A Chicagoan, he would play six years in the major leagues with Philadelphia (National League), the St. Louis Browns, the Chicago White Sox and the Cincinnati Reds. In 1906, he was traded by the Browns to Milwaukee of the American Association for another catcher, Branch Rickey. Roth hit a single home run in 783 major-league plate appearances over six seasons.

Formation of the NAPBL

New territorial wars led to major-league raids on minor-league players. The minors forged another agreement for their own self-protection. The National Association of Professional Baseball Leagues (NAPBL) was officially founded at a September 1901 meeting in Chicago. Three-I League president Sexton played a significant role in its establishment. The NAPBL remains but was renamed Minor League Baseball (MiLB) in 1999.

An important provision of the agreement was the classification of all minor leagues. Every minor league in organized baseball was classified alphabetically, A through D, with A being the highest designation at inception of the agreement.

Evansville joined the NAPBL with an entry into the Class-B Three-I League. The River Rats finished sixth out of eight teams.

Larry Schaffley, outfielder for the 1901 River Rats. He later managed the Federal League's Buffalo Buffeds. *Author's collection.*

PITCHING APLENTY: NEW JERSEY IMPORTS

In June, southpaw pitcher and New Jersey native Frederick Bruchell tossed a ten-inning no-hitter against Bloomington (Illinois), ending the League Park game in dramatic fashion. A right-handed batsman, Bruchell knocked in the lone run of the game with a triple. Bruchell was in the big leagues the next year with the Phillies and spent parts of three seasons with the Boston Red Sox.

Parker Treat, a twenty-two-year-old right-hander from Morristown, New Jersey, celebrated the Fourth of July by mowing down homestanding Terre Haute without a hit in the second game of a doubleheader. Treat threw his 1–0 gem in front of 2,200 mostly hostile Tot fans. The festive crowd included an Evansville contingent that featured 500 "rooters" who came north on a morning train for the holiday doubleheader.

"The echoes of pistols and cannons and other holiday pandemonium makers were resounding in the ears of the young pitcher," wrote *Courier* reporter Dr. Wallace C. Dyer. Dr. Dyer was believed to be the first bylined reporter for the newspaper. Besides excelling at writing and practicing medicine, Dyer earned a law degree. He later rose to the rank of lieutenant colonel in World War I.

"But as fifth, sixth, seventh, eighth, and finally ninth inning passed without a hit the hostile crowd was changed to admirers of the clever and sturdy youngster," wrote Dyer. Treat spent six years in the minor leagues and never made it to the majors.

Treat was on the opposite end of a one-hitter at Cedar Rapids in August. Despite the loss, Treat witnessed his fielders back him in the most flawless way in the fourth inning. With Cedar Rapids runners on first and second, their batter hit a line drive straight into the hands of River Rats second baseman Frank Quinn. The baserunners were off at the crack of the bat, so Quinn threw to first baseman Tom News, who turned and threw back to shortstop Charles Ebert before the runner could get back.

PARK TREAT.

Parker Treat tossed a July 4 no-hitter against the Terre Haute Tots in 1902. *Author's collection.*

The Central League

GALLERY OF CENTRAL LEAGUE NOTABLES

SECOND BASEMAN BONNOR.

River Rats second baseman John Bonner led the 1903 Central League in batting. *Author's collection.*

The River Rats jumped to the Central League from 1903 to 1911. Evansville club president and resident George William Bement was appointed league president. After Bement took charge, a bill was presented to the Indiana State legislature that allowed baseball to be played on Sundays after 2:00 p.m.

The River Rats finished fifth in the eight-team league with a 64-68 record. Rival Terre Haute ended dead last. Evansville second baseman John Bonner was the circuit's batting champ with a .328 average on 172 hits. Bonner was sold to Atlanta prior to the final game of the season. Fort Wayne won the pennant.

The next year was lackluster, both on the field and in the pocketbook. The club floundered on the field and at the turnstiles and disbanded in early September when president George Bement said that finishing the season would mean considerable financial loss that he was not willing to meet alone. The club forfeited its final six games.

Bement resigned as Central League president and began a campaign to return Evansville to the league. Dr. Frank Carson of South Bend replaced him as league head. Bement issued a circular letter asking for subscriptions of not more than $10 and not less than $5 to purchase the club at a minimum cost of $500. His reasons for wishing to keep organized baseball in Evansville were stated in the letter:

> *First—That league baseball is a clean summer sport desired by the masses.*
> *Second—That league baseball is an advertisement of Evansville throughout the United States.*
> *Third—That the dropping of Evansville from the circuit of the Central League would rather reflect* [poorly] *upon a progressive city.*

ROUGHHOUSE RYAN

Bement and John P. Walker formed a stock company to help foot the bill for 1905. A well-known baseball man joined them and was named field manager. Jimmy Ryan was a household name to major-league fans of the day. Ryan played mostly for Chicago teams (White Stockings, Colts, and Orphans) from 1885 to 1903. His career ended with a lifetime .308 average, 2,502 hits, 118 home runs, 1,093 runs batted in and 419 stolen bases. Ryan, known for his surly disposition, was generally not well liked by teammates.

Evansville finished fourth in the eight-team circuit. As a player, Ryan slugged 10 home runs to lead the Central League. Now forty-two years old, he also hit .311 as an outfielder. The 1906 club slumped and settled into the middle of the Central League pack halfway through the season. Frustration came to a head during a July 19 home game against Springfield when Ryan let a spectator get the best of him.

In the third inning, Jimmy went into the stands and "escorted" a man out of League Park, ripping his shirt. Ryan claimed the individual was "hurling slurring personal remarks" at him and his team. The exiting fan claimed that he wasn't the perpetrator. Some in attendance agreed that Ryan had the wrong guy. Others near the scene took Ryan's side.

The spectator said he would consider prosecuting Ryan. After speaking with attorneys, he entered a $20,000 suit against Ryan. The verdict didn't come until early March of the next year. The suit was dismissed, the judge holding that "baseball management has the privilege of ejecting spectators who unreasonably jeer and hoot at umpires or players." No matter. Amid complaints about his management style, Ryan and Evansville management agreed to part ways on July 28, 1906. Ryan, accompanied by his wife, left quietly by train back to Chicago.

"Long" Tom Letcher, a veteran of sixteen minor-league seasons and an outfielder on the team, replaced Ryan. Letcher was popular with the fans. His selection looked like a brilliant choice. In the new skipper's first day at the helm, Rats pitcher James Freeman delighted a crowd of nearly three thousand who had "crammed and jammed their way into League Park." Freeman tossed a 2–0 no-hitter at rival Terre Haute.

The pitcher nicknamed "Buck" was magnificent, albeit slightly wild. He stymied Terre Haute despite walking seven and hitting one. A fielding gem by second baseman Charlie French in the eighth inning saved Freeman's gem. French made a running one-handed stab of a ground ball headed for right field, whirled, threw and nipped the runner at first. Freeman won

The 1907 River Rats with League Park grandstands in the background. *Courtesy of Willard Library Archives.*

twenty-two games for the River Rats in 1906 and led the Central League with 214 strikeouts. Freeman never played in the majors.

The enthusiasm surrounding Letcher died quickly. On September 14, a relieved Letcher was removed as manager and replaced by catcher Charles F. "Nig" Fuller and later Harry Stahlhefer. Evansville finished thirty-two games out of first place behind Grand Rapids.

Before the 1907 season, Stahlhefer put together a group of investors and bought the team from county treasurer and club president John Walker. Club president Stahlhefer found a new manager in Charles Elmer "Punch" Knoll, who gained his release from New Orleans of the Southern League to take the helm. Punch was one year removed from playing in the big leagues with Washington. He still played the outfield. Central League stalwart Springfield ran away with the 1907 title. A more stable Evansville ended up in the middle of the standings under Knoll.

The First Pennant

The first professional baseball championship silenced Evansville critics in 1908. The River Rats captured the Central League pennant as eighty-six thousand people poured into League Park during the seventy-game home season.

Knoll led the circuit in home runs with 12. Pitcher Charles James "Demon Jimmy" Wacker made the most headlines. He posted a 27-8 record to establish the Evansville professional record for wins in a season. The southpaw won 17 games for the 1906 River Rats but sat out most of 1907 after suffering acute appendicitis in early May. Wacker tried to play early that season, until he was taken to St. Mary's Hospital in the third week of May, where he laid in bed for a week before finally undergoing surgery to remove the organ. Wacker emerged from surgery in "very critical condition." The doctor's prognosis was grim. After three weeks at St. Mary's, his fever subsided. Wacker made a full recovery leading into his record-setting season.

Punch Knoll spent nearly thirty years managing and playing in the minor leagues. He collected over 2,400 hits in his minor-league playing career. In his single major-league season, 1905, he hit .213 in seventy-nine games for the Washington Senators. In twenty-two years as a minor-league manager, Punch amassed a record of 1,479 wins and 1,317 losses. Knoll won four other league championships—two while managing Bay City (Michigan) in the Michigan-Ontario League and one each with Fort Wayne (Central League) and Dayton (Central).

Central League champions of 1908. This was Evansville's first professional pennant-winning team. *Courtesy of University of Southern Indiana.*

WITH THE PLAYERS DURING THE OFF SEASON—No. 1

By K. K. Knecht, the Cartoonist.

Courier artist Karl K. Knecht drew
Punch Knoll in January 1909.
Evansville Courier & Press.

After baseball, Knoll retired to an orchard and a farm near Chandler,
Indiana. He was referred to as "Mr. Baseball" in southwestern Indiana.
Born in Evansville (1881), Punch died in his hometown in 1960.

The 1909 Evansville club came back to earth, finishing second to last
in the Central League. Wheeling (West Virginia) ran away with the crown.
Evansville hitters Knoll and Hank Butcher tied for the home run crown with
11 each. After the season, Knoll left Evansville to take the manager's job in
Dayton, also in the Central League. Angus Grant, a second baseman from
South Bend, took Knoll's place as manager for the 1910 season.

Cobb Stops By

Ty Cobb and the Detroit Tigers visited Louisiana Street Park for two
exhibition games in early April 1910. The *Courier* reported that Cobb joined

the team in Evansville after failing to meet up with them a few days earlier in Louisville. Ty claimed, "Business had been so brisk that he had a time getting everything in readiness to start the season." Cobb made millions in business largely through his investments in such companies as General Motors and Coca-Cola.

Cobb had already earned the universal reputation as a dirty player, but the *Courier* reported that Cobb didn't look so ferocious. "Yesterday [at the workout] he actually passed several players without biting a one," reported the paper. Cobb went 1-4 in his appearance in Evansville before a reported crowd of eight hundred at the Louisiana Street Ball Park. The Tigers beat Evansville, 5–4, in a little less than two hours.

STERZER AND CRISTALL

River Rats lefty Carl "Buck" Sterzer won 28 games in 1910 to set the all-time season record, erasing Wacker's mark of 27. Sterzer won 28 games again in 1914 pitching for St. Joseph (Michigan) in the Western League. "Buck" pitched nine professional seasons and never made it above Class-A ball. The River Rats finished in fourth place behind winner South Bend.

The best-pitched game of the 1910 season was turned in by lefty Bill Cristall. Cristall was a journeyman who ended up toiling for seventeen years in the minors. He was born in Odessa, Russia, in the Ukraine in 1878. Bill was one of only three Ukrainians in baseball history. He was also Jewish.

The southpaw tossed nine full innings of no-hit ball against Grand Rapids at League Park. The score after nine innings was 0–0. Grand Rapids finally got its first hit with two outs in the tenth. Cristall calmly fanned the next batter to get out of the inning. It all fell apart in the eleventh. Bill hit a batter and threw a wild pitch that allowed the runner to take second. The runner then stole third and scored on a grounder to second base. Grand Rapids won, 1–0. Cristall struck out 11 and walked 2.

EVANSVILLE'S LARRY LEGEND

A more seasoned River Rat became a national sports celebrity after the 1910 season. He established a baseball record that would stand for over forty years. Outfielder Sheldon Aldenburg "Larry" Lejeune had just finished a spectacular season, leading the Central League in hitting at .328 and in home runs with 18. He also tallied the league's most runs (81), total bases (244) and stolen bases (54). Lejeune was courted by Brooklyn of the National League for his overall baseball talent.

The twenty-four-year-old Larry Lejeune had one overriding ambition: to make the longest throw in baseball history. He competed in the long-throw competition of Cincinnati's annual Field Day in October. The distance throwing record going into the competition stood at 400 feet, 7-1/2 inches, set by John Hatfield in 1874. Lejeune held the unofficial record for "league" ballplayers. He threw the horsehide 399 feet, 10-3/4 inches in competition while with Springfield in the Central League in 1907.

Lejeune's first two throws were barely over 385 feet "against the wind." Frustrated by the conditions, he "asked permission" to throw in the opposite direction. The referee granted Lejeune's request. On his next throw, the Evansville outfielder unleashed a 401-foot, 4½-inch bomb. Not satisfied, Lejeune asked to throw one more. With a running start, Lejeune rifled the ball 426 feet, 9½ inches.

The story made national headlines. After setting the record, Larry purchased a tavern at 116 Locust Street in Evansville. The establishment, the Home Run Saloon, featured former River Rats pitcher Jimmy Wacker as bartender. The major leagues came calling. Larry held out when Brooklyn offered a contract for $225 per month. He wanted $275 or he'd consider staying in Evansville. Lejeune got $275. Before heading to Brooklyn in late March, an automobile in which he was a passenger with three others got caught between a streetcar and a carriage and crashed into a telegraph pole. Lejeune was badly bruised but sustained no fractures.

A slow start in Brooklyn sent him back to Chattanooga of the Southern League early in the season. His career spanned ten minor-league seasons. The last was 1916. Lejeune led leagues in batting average five times as a minor-leaguer but was plagued by injuries throughout his career. He made it back to the majors with Pittsburgh in 1915.

RATS REMOVED

Don Parker replaced Angus Grant as River Rats manager midyear. The Grand Rapids club moved to Newark in June. South Bend relocated to

Grand Rapids in July. Evansville transferred to South Bend in August and was renamed the "Benders" by order of Central League president Dr. Frank Carson, a South Bend resident. The home white uniforms stayed in Evansville. League Park's groundskeeper locked them up until he was paid ninety-seven dollars owed to him.

The South Bend move turned out badly. It cost the league additional expense of $3,000, a sum equal to the cost of a typical franchise. Later estimates were much higher. South Bend attendance slumped, and creditors deprived the Benders the use of the South Bend ballpark for the last three days of the season, "owing to back rent." The events of 1911 left Evansville without a Central League berth.

The Class-D Kitty League came calling. Kitty League president C.C. Gosnell visited Evansville, but other league members weren't sure Evansville was a fit. They complained that a city the size of Evansville (population 70,000) frequently violated salary limits when in leagues with smaller towns. They feared that added bonuses would secure better players and ensure a pennant winner, damaging attendance in the other cities. Conversely, Evansville considered Class-D an insult to a city of its size.

The Kitty League was still courting Evansville in February when the courtship soured. Central League president Frank Carson demanded compensation from the Kitty League, maintaining that he owned territorial rights to professional baseball in Evansville. Carson claimed it cost the Central League $5,000 to prop up the franchise he moved to South Bend. The Kitty League said it would pay nothing.

As April approached, Dr. Frank Bassett, a wealthy Hopkinsville physician, replaced Gosnell as Kitty League president. Bassett and Central League head Frank Carson took the territorial rights issue to Cincinnati, where the secretary of the National Association established $1,000 as the price for the Kitty League to obtain rights. Dr. Bassett paid the bill. The deal included provisions favorable to Evansville. Bassett said that Evansville could leave for no charge if it found a better league at the conclusion of the season. League Park was secured for ten Sunday home games and doubleheaders on Memorial Day, July 4 and Labor Day. Two league members—Hopkinsville and Clarksville—did not permit Sunday games.

A new Evansville Baseball Association was incorporated to sell $5,000 of stock in the club. Club directors were led by local furniture company entrepreneur Benjamin Bosse. He threw out the first pitch on Opening Day with hopes that the Kitty League would lead to bigger things.

Yankees: One Year in the Kitty League

Baseball in Evansville barely survived in the Class-D Kentucky-Illinois-Tennessee League as the Evansville Yankees. The lower class was an embarrassment to city dwellers; at midseason, attendance wasn't good. There was little hope of moving to a higher league. But geography made travel easier in this league. Neighboring Henderson was a rival. Paducah and Hopkinsville were other nearby Kentucky teams. Cairo was the lone Illinois entry. Clarksville was Tennessee's.

After a sparsely attended Friday game in July, Bosse issued a statement that management "did not care to lose any more money." Without marked improvement in the next two days, there would be no more baseball in Evansville after Sunday, said Bosse. The Yankees made it through the weekend without folding, so Bosse organized a last-ditch effort to save baseball with two "booster" games the following week. The first yielded the largest weekday crowd of the season. The second, the following Sunday, drew more than two thousand to a doubleheader against Hopkinsville. The franchise was saved, and the prospect of a better league was alive. The Evansville Yankees stumbled to a third-place finish with a record of 47-52.

The downgrade from Class B to D was a springboard event for a future Hall of Famer. Edd Roush of Oakland City, Indiana, started his professional career as a Yankee, batting .284.

A Team of Color: The Maroons

While interest in the Class-D team waned, a local "colored" team, the Evansville Maroons, drew large crowds. The Maroons were a barnstorming independent group of players from Louisville and Chicago. Local papers touted the Maroons and their opponents, saying the "brand of ball they are putting up is ahead of some seen in minor league games."

The Maroons played home games in League Park, East End Park and a new park that could be reached from the Oak Hill car line (near Oak Hill Cemetery). Car lines were electric streetcars with routes to many areas around Evansville. Many "colored" barnstorming teams made Evansville a destination to play the Maroons while touring the country. Among them were Brooklyn's Royal Giants, Chicago's Union Giants, Cleveland's Syndicates, Louisville's Tigers, Memphis' Tigers and Pensacola's Giants.

The *Journal-News* called Brooklyn "champions of all of colored baseball in the East." Maroon games at League Park regularly outdrew the Yankees when that team was playing elsewhere. One Maroon game against the Pensacola Giants in May was highlighted by an unassisted triple play. The visiting team's first baseman, named Ward, pulled off the feat "before a big crowd of fans."

SOUTH BEND SHENANIGANS

The charge back to the Central League was led by Harry Stahlhefer. Stahlhefer attempted to buy failing franchises like Terre Haute and South Bend, but the indiscretions of 1911 lingered as roadblocks. Financial claims against Evansville remained from the calamity. It was believed that then Central League president Dr. Frank Carson (a resident of South Bend) and then Evansville manager Angus Grant put Evansville behind the eight ball.

Stahlhefer filed an application to enter the Central League but came back from league meetings empty-handed. South Bend newspapers began writing disparaging articles about Evansville. The *Courier* responded on its editorial page, claiming, "Evansville has never been the chronic charge upon baseball that South Bend has been." The editorial took pokes at former president Carson, pointing to his bias as an impediment to Evansville.

The bickering spilled into 1913, when the issues were handed to the National Baseball Commission in Cincinnati to review. Its report exonerated Evansville. Commissioners ordered an adjustment of claims against the club to the sum of $1,500.00 from the original claim amount of $2,142.95. The commission then ordered the Central League to pay the claim and advised the claimants and citizens to petition to annul the sale of its Class-B Central League team to the Class-D Kitty League. The petition was granted. That paved the way for the Central League to award a franchise to Evansville.

During the investigation, commissioners also discovered that cash receipts of the 1911 club exceeded disbursements by $5,000 and the difference had not been accounted for. Led by then president Carson, the league took over the franchise and moved it to South Bend, purportedly because of its dire financial position. The assertion appeared ludicrous.

"The decision of the National Commission upholds practically all the contentions of the local [creditors] and shows both former President Carson of the Central and former Manager Angus Grant in no enviable light," wrote the *Courier*. "The statement that the Grants have made no explanation of the use to which they put $5,000 above disbursements they made may be embarrassing to them should either [Carson or Grant] attempt to get into organized baseball again." Angus Grant, also a South Bend resident, never again played, coached or managed in organized baseball. Dr. Carson never returned to organized baseball

Stahlhefer received signed papers from league president Louie Heilbroner granting the franchise. Heilbroner had been appointed Central League president in 1912.

EDD ROUSH

Evansville returned as the River Rats. After twenty-four years of use, the wood ballpark on Louisiana Street was decaying, and the nearby stockyards wanted to expand. High winds nearly destroyed the amphitheater grandstands midway through the season. The damage required schedule changes while repairs were made. Additionally, a historic flood put much of the Ohio Valley underwater. The Ohio River crested at about forty-eight feet, thirteen feet above established flood levels near Evansville. Scheduled exhibition games prior to the season were canceled, but the field was ready for the late-April season opener.

Punch Knoll returned as manager after three years in Dayton. Knoll was sold to Dayton for the sum of $650 in 1910. Stahlhefer paid Dayton roughly the same amount to bring him back. Republican mayor Charles Heilman threw out the first pitch to open the season against Grand Rapids. Every politically connected male in town was among more than 3,400 in attendance, including the next mayor, Benjamin Bosse.

Knoll's club was plagued by early injuries and never recovered. The River Rats finished 1913 in last place, winning just 60 of 140 games. Edd Roush was batting .325 when club president Harry Stahlhefer sold him to Charles Comiskey's Chicago White Sox in August. The renowned tightwad Comiskey signed Roush for $3,000 per year.

Roush found a home with the Cincinnati Reds. He won the National League batting crown in 1917 and again during the team's World Series championship year of 1919. He was elected to the Baseball Hall of Fame in 1962 with a .323 lifetime major-league batting average on 2,376 hits. He also hit 182 triples, which still ranks fifteenth all-time. Cincinnati fans voted Roush "The Greatest Red Who Ever Lived" in 1969.

FITTERY THE FLINGER

Pitching took the spotlight from Roush on August 6, 1913, when one of the most prolific pitchers in minor-league history, Paul Fittery, tossed a gem for the River Rats in Terre Haute. "With a world of speed and everything else needed in the repertoire of a flinger, the southpaw made Terrier batters blink 29 times, the results of which was nary a hit for the local batsmen."

One error and one walk accounted for the only Terre Haute baserunners in Fittery's 5–0 no-hit masterpiece. With manager Punch Knoll in center field and Roush in right, the outfield saw only six balls leave the infield. Second baseman Frank Mathews made a third inning barehanded catch over his head to prevent the only thing close to a hit.

It was another win in a career that totaled 294 in Fittery's eighteen minor-league seasons. He won over 20 games in a season five times, with a high mark of 29 for Salt Lake City in the Pacific Coast League in 1916. His 2,359 career strikeouts put him tenth all-time among minor-league pitchers. Fittery's 1913 record was an ordinary 13-12. He came back the next year to post a stellar 22-7 mark for the River Rats and led the Central League in strikeouts with 249 for the second-place team. The gaudy numbers caught the attention of the Cincinnati Reds, who purchased him late in the season.

Evansville finished eight and one-half games behind pennant-winning Dayton.

THE FIELD DAY OPPORTUNITY

League Park hosted civic events when the River Rats were on the road. During the closing minutes of the highly attended annual school Field Day Pageant on May 22, 1914, a section of the park's temporary stands collapsed. In the crackup, 42 people were injured, some seriously. More than 8,000 people witnessed the destruction, which made front-page news for days. Among the crowd were about 1,800 kids from the Evansville school system going through Field Day exercises. Miraculously, none of the 42 died of injuries directly related to the collapse. Lawsuits resulting from the collapse were adjudicated into the 1920s, with plaintiffs unsuccessful in every case. The collapse was the beginning of the end to the rotting ballpark.

Knecht's recollection of League Park. Evansville Courier & Press.

The Louisiana Street Park annually hosted Field Day for Evansville schools. *Courtesy of Willard Library Archives.*

Mayor Benjamin Bosse saw opportunity in the event and seized the moment. Bosse had ideas for the Evansville minor-league team, in which he had an ownership interest. His vision revolved around eighty acres of land the city had acquired for $50,000 from heirs of local attorney Thomas Garvin less than thirty days into his first term. Bosse envisioned a new facility that could be used for school activities, athletic events, civic activities and Field Day. He wanted something that could also be used as a ballpark. Local architect Harry E. Boyle was hired to design such a place. Boyle's work is seen today around Evansville with buildings of such diverse designs as the old Central Library and the Pagoda at Sunset Park Pavilion, among others.

Bosse convinced the board of education to build a multipurpose stadium in an area of Garvin Park on the city's north side. The board approved the project at an estimated cost of $40,000. By doing so, the city made a commitment no other U.S. municipality had. Evansville funded the building of an athletic field as a school board project. The M.J. Hoffman Construction Company was hired to build the Boyle design.

School board members included Charles Enlow, Daniel Wertz, Howard Roosa and Abraham Strouse. Roosa, the *Courier's* editor, was appointed to the board by Bosse. Wertz and Roosa now have Evansville elementary schools named after them. Enlow Field, built in 1926, is still vibrantly standing on the grounds of Bosse High School and still bears his name.

THE FIELD

Mayor Bosse and city officials boasted that the venue would be the most magnificent minor-league stadium in the country and could be used for football and other sports. "Evansville is blazing a trail out of minor league difficulties and showing the way to the baseball world," proclaimed Central League president Louis Heilbroner, "and there is nothing else approaching it in the minor league world."

Newspapers around the nation covered the first-ever undertaking. Bosse hinted to reporters that municipal ownership of the field was just the beginning. "If I find that the law permits a city to enter upon municipal ownership of baseball," Bosse was quoted, "I shall be in favor of the city's taking over the Evansville

Evansville mayor Benjamin Bosse led construction of the first municipally owned sports facility in history. *Courtesy Willard Library Archives.*

Central League team." Bosse was vice-president of the club and shared controlling interest in the team.

"Municipal Baseball to Save the Minor Leagues" headlined a story in the *Shreveport Times*. Most, if not all, newspapers across the country jumped the gun. Municipal ownership of the team never materialized. Nonetheless, city ownership of a stadium was the talk of the baseball world.

Opening Day

The field was named Bosse Field, for the mayor who would go on to serve from 1914 to 1922. Bosse, a progressive, was Evansville's first three-term mayor. Proving true his motto "When everybody boosts, everybody wins," Bosse Field opened on June 17, 1915, for a game against Erie. Before the game, a band marched from Sunset Park, near the Ohio River, to Garvin Park on the north side, where the field sat on ten acres of land. Seating capacity was listed at 7,180, but 8,082 people turned out for the first game, a 4–0 River Rats win. It was the largest crowd in Central League history.

The original stadium was a concrete "fireproof" edifice. The land, materials, labor and city fees brought the total cost to roughly $65,000.

Bosse Field's exterior was not red brick until renovations were made in 1930. *Courtesy of Willard Library Archives.*

Above: Panoramic portrait before the first game at Bosse Field. *Courtesy of Willard Library Archives.*

Opposite, middle: The hustle and bustle of game day at the new field. *Courtesy of Willard Library Archives.*

Opposite, bottom: Batting practice at Bosse Field. *Courtesy of Willard Library Archives.*

Benjamin Bosse died in 1922 of rheumatism, complications of influenza, pneumonia and heart trouble while still in office. He owned the *Evansville Courier* from 1920 until his death. The River Rats won the Central League title by four games. The 1915 pennant clincher came on August 23 with a 6–0 win over the rival Terre Haute "Tots." This unattributed poem was part of the *Courier* game story the following day:

> We've clinched the flag,
> We've copped the rag,
> The bunting is ours;
> Hip, Hip, Hooray, turn out today
> To see the Eva champions play.

Construction of Bosse Field was validated in 1916. Field Day exercises made a profit of $1,500. The net profit from the 1914 Field Day was $971. Nearly 8,500 city residents attended the festivities. Field Day was a rousing success, but the baseball club, now called the Evansville Evas, was lackluster. They ended 1916 in the middle of the Central League pack at fifth place.

No-Hit City

The 1916 season highlight belonged to tall Spencer County right-hander Frank Winchell, who had been a member of the 1912 Evansville Yankees. Winchell hurled an almost perfect game on August 3. One batter reached first base as Winchell faced only twenty-eight batters, no-hitting the Springfield Reapers, 1–0. The lone baserunner came on a throwing error. Only four balls reached outfielders. Winchell struck out six. Manager Knoll played right field.

Another fifth-place finish by Evansville followed in 1917. Grand Rapids swept the regular-season title and won the playoffs over Peoria. The year featured another no-hit game.

Knoll manned right field while tall right-hander Tom Kernaghan mowed down homestanding South Bend before a Bender crowd of 2,100 on May 13. Four South Bend hitters reached base in a brilliant 1–0 Evansville win that, at the time, put the River Rats in first place with a 6-2 record. "Kerny" had signed in the fall of 1916. Three balls were hit to outfielders, as twenty-four of the twenty-seven outs were handled by Evansville infielders.

The First World War

Evansville baseball paused during the 1918 season. The city was not alone in shuttering its hardball teams. The United States entered the war in Europe. Attempts to hold the Central League together vanished in March 1918 due to lack of interest from enough existing member cities. Terre Haute and cities from Illinois and Missouri tried to promote a new league made up of the ravaged Central and Three-I circuits. Evansville was invited, but Stahlhefer refused to consider the propositions.

The minor leagues were down to just nine leagues at the start of the season. By the end of the baseball year, only the Class-AA International League had completed a full schedule. Players and coaches went to war or on to other ventures. Punch Knoll sat out the year and operated a tavern at the corner of Governor Street and Green River Road in Evansville.

3

A NEW BEGINNING, DEPRESSION AND LIGHTS OUT

1919–31

THE NEW THREE-EYE

The minors fired up when the war ended in September 1918. A new club was officially named the Evansville Black Sox and joined the new Three-I League. League president Albert R. Tearney recruited teams from the old Central to join a few Three-I holdovers. Tearney was a frequent visitor to Evansville and pushed to get the city in his league. Tearney said Bosse Field was a big reason he wanted the city in.

The league contained teams from Peoria, Evansville, Terre Haute, Moline, Bloomington and Rockford. The two Indiana teams came from the old Central League, although Terre Haute wasn't active in the year before the war. The rest were returning to the Three-I. Each put up a $2,000 stake before the start of the 120-game season.

Rosters were limited to thirteen players—seven infielders or outfielders, four pitchers, one regular catcher and one substitute catcher. If the manager was a player, the limit would allow fourteen players. Manager Johnny Nee served as the team's second baseman and led the league in runs scored.

The Black Sox opened 1919 with a 6–4 win over Terre Haute. More than two thousand attended to see the Browns, managed by Mordecai Brown. Brown also took his place in the pitching rotation in the coming year. "Three Finger" still had some stuff. At forty-two years old, he accounted for sixteen of Terre Haute's fifty wins. Umpiring the first game of the new season was

A packed house view from the first-base line. *Courtesy of Willard Library Archives.*

Karl K. Knecht, the *Courier*'s official photographer, shown on the field. *Courtesy of the University of Southern Indiana.*

Mr. Fan, Do You Want Baseball This Year? If You Do, Clip This Coupon and Send It In

I, ..., the un-

dersigned, subscribe to (   ) shares of capital

stock for the **Evansville Fans' Association** at $10 per share.

Signed ....

Address ....

Make checks payable to Evansville Fans' Association. Mail to sporting editor of The Journal-News.

A stock offering helped finance the new Evansville Black Sox Club after World War I.
Author's collection.

another familiar face, Frank Roth. The former River Rat slugger had retired from playing after the 1913 season.

The Black Sox finished third behind Bloomington and Peoria. Veteran pitcher Frank Winchell tossed his second no-hit game in an Evansville uniform on August 23 against the Moline Plowboys. Winchell is the only pitcher in Evansville professional baseball history to pitch more than one no-hitter. Winchell struck out 4 and walked 1 in the 2–0 Bosse Field masterpiece. Punch Knoll, who had played right field in Winchell's 1916 no-hitter, backed him up again by chasing down two fly-ball outs in left field. It was Knoll's fourth appearance as a player in a no-hit game by an Evansville hurler.

Evas and Little Evas

The team was reborn as the Evansville Evas in 1920. Johnny Nee left Evansville for a manager's job in San Antonio. Career minor-leaguer Lew Groh took his first job as a skipper. Groh planned to play shortstop and made his first move by signing second baseman Lee Meyers from Nashville of the Southern Association. Groh also gave a tryout to Syl Simon of Evansville. Simon, an amateur infielder, didn't make the Evas but caught the eye of Ludington (Michigan) manager Punch Knoll and played there in 1920. It was the beginning of an association that would last a lifetime for the two men.

By midyear, a slumping Evansville team fell eight and one-half games behind Bloomington. Groh resigned amid reports he was not getting along with players. Al Bashang, the team's popular center fielder, took his place. The Evas won forty of their final sixty-one games under Bashang and finished in second place. Bashang signed a new contract after an extraordinary amount of haggling. The Evas slipped to fifth place in 1921, and Bashang was gone.

Johnny Nee returned to manage in 1922 and was delighted to be back. The season was a mild success, as his crew edged out Rockford for fourth place. Nee also played and hit .335. Foster "Babe" Ganzel hit .326 as a twenty-one-year-old rookie outfielder and third baseman. Ganzel played eighteen years in the minors and parts of two seasons with the Washington Senators before ending his playing career after the 1942 season. Eva second baseman Pete Hughes set the professional record for sacrifice hits in a season, laying down 75.

The 1922 Evas manager, Johnny Nee, is at far right in the back row. *Courtesy of Willard Library Archives.*

The Eva name had evolved to Evansville Little Evas, much to the dismay of G.A. Beard, president of the Evansville Fans Association. So, Beard conducted a contest to rename the team in March 1924. Contestants were restricted to names of ten letters or fewer. The winner received thirty game tickets for the upcoming season. The name Evansville Pocketeers was unanimously selected. Three submissions tied as contest winners, according to the *Courier*. The winners were Howard E. Jones and a "modest" Mr. H.H., both of 716 Walnut Street, and G.W. Surlls of the Deakin Apartments. All three received thirty grandstand tickets. The newspaper reported that some submissions touched a tone of comedy, while others were "totally unsuitable."

Dunn's Dilemmas

Johnny Nee left for a managerial job with Augusta (Georgia) of the South Atlantic League. Nee was replaced by Joe Dunn. Dunn was the full-time catcher on the 1908 Central League pennant-winning River Rats. Players liked Dunn. Pocketeers third sacker Paddy Reagan led the Three-I in hitting with a .329 average. He also led the circuit in hits, runs and home runs, falling short of the league Triple Crown in the RBI column.

Dunn's first season was tumultuous. His troubles started at a mid-June homestand against the Bloomington Bloomers. After a one-run loss, Evansville fans swarmed the field and rushed two umpires, named Hopper and Taylor. Hopper was shaken but not hurt. Police subdued the crowd. Dunn was in the locker room during the kerfuffle. The next day, a Sunday, Dunn received a no-nonsense telegram from A.R. Tearney, Three-I League president in Chicago, saying:

> *After yesterday's affair there is nothing left for me to do other than place the*
> *blame entirely upon you. There is no use to communicate with me.*
> *Get ready to leave the league.*
> [Signed] *A.R. Tearney*

Fans lined up to support Dunn. The *Courier* sent a telegram to Tearney blaming the umpires. Beard assumed that Tearney's information source was umpire Robert Taylor, who had left for Chicago following the game. G.A. Beard traveled to Chicago to meet with Tearney on Wednesday. By Friday, Tearney issued a statement absolving Dunn of blame. Tearney told Beard that Taylor had exaggerated his story. Tearney received upward of forty telegrams and a "basketful" of letters from Evansville fans telling "the real story." Dunn was suspended again in mid-July after a game at Decatur in which he protested an umpire's decision. He was again reinstated by Tearney.

The race for another pennant came down to the last day of the season, with the Pocketeers needing a win over Bloomington and a Terre Haute loss to Danville to win the pennant. Neither happened, and the club finished one game behind the Bloomington Bloomers. Dunn's leadership was good enough to be retained for 1925.

Death and Drama

The Three-I League adapted the practice of putting numbers on player jerseys in 1925. The 1925 Pocketeers held down third place going into the morning game of a home Labor Day doubleheader against the Decatur Commies. Dunn had a solid rotation with Charles Barnabe, Charles Fulton, Elmer Gray and Earnest Regenold. Barnabe ended with 22 wins on the year. Fulton chipped in with 16. Gray had 10 wins. Regenold was known as the Pocketeers' hard-luck pitcher but tossed 234 innings for the year.

Gray was nursing a sore arm but started game one. After a scoreless first inning, the Commies got to him. Gray normally threw overhanded but was side-arming his pitches due to soreness. The sixth batter in the second inning was Decatur pitcher Louis Chedo, a promising recent signee. With a runner on first base, Chedo squared to bunt. The bunt attempt went awry.

Gray's pitch sailed. Chedo tried to duck out of the way but appeared to move directly into the ball. The ball hit his temple so hard that it bounded to first base. Gray rushed to the downed batsmen. After a time, and to the relief of Gray, Chedo was assisted to the dugout by two teammates. Gray was the first to the dugout to shake Chedo's hand, in visible relief that he appeared okay. A tired Gray was relieved by Earnest Regenold as the Pocketeers went on to lose. Chedo got credit for the win.

Dr. C.W. Hartloff of Evansville took the injured pitcher to the office of Dr. Walter Cleveland, an X-ray specialist. No fracture was detected, so Chedo was transported to his room at the Vendome Hotel. Dr. Hartloff left him around 11:00 a.m., instructing Vendome employees to phone him if Chedo got worse. Hartloff said he would be back around 4:00 p.m. Shortly after 1:00 p.m., Hartloff's phone rang. It was the Vendome. Chedo was not doing well. An ambulance transported Chedo to St. Mary's Hospital, where a brain hemorrhage was detected. Dr. Edwin Long commenced surgery on Chedo around 3:00 p.m. The twenty-three-year-old died around 1:00 a.m.

A somber Elmer Gray was informed later that morning. A next-day investigation by coroner Max Lowe absolved Gray of blame and declared the death an accident. A blood clot on the brain that surgery could not relieve was the cause of the pitcher's death. Lowe's investigation included testimony from Gray, Dunn, G.A. Beard, umpire Charles Shaffer and catcher Ansel Leibrook.

The *Daily Illinois State Journal*, a Springfield paper, reported, "Commie players to a man stated that Elmer Gray was in no way responsible for the unfortunate accident." Gray was considered a gentleman and sportsman in the Three-I. He had played for Decatur in 1923. The funeral took place on September 11 in Chedo's hometown of Christopher, Illinois. One of seven brothers, he was a baseball idol in that area. The *Decatur Herald* said it was largest crowd to attend the funeral of a private citizen in the history of southern Illinois. Nearly one thousand people saw a "flower mountain" cover his casket. At 2:00 p.m., the Three-I League stopped for a moment of silence while last rites were given.

Skipper Stanage

The Pocketeers finished third in 1925, and the Fans Association, led by G.A. Beard, announced that a "house cleaning" was forthcoming. Owners lost around $6,000 over the previous four years. Dunn shuffled off to Elmira, New York, for a manager's job, and Beard looked for a new skipper. Some thirty applications came in for the job. Beard aimed high and got what he wanted, a major-leaguer: Oscar Stanage.

Stanage had been a longtime major-league catcher who served as a coach under Detroit manager Ty Cobb in 1925. Stanage earned the respect of Cobb, an honor few attained. Stanage was with Detroit from 1909 to 1920 and appeared in one World Series (1909). Stanage feared little and stood up to Cobb very early in his career. Cobb was known to seek out Stanage as a partner when fights broke out. Stanage caught in 86 games for Evansville and batted .251 at age forty-three.

The housecleaning continued through the winter and spring as Stanage worked to put together a new ball club. Beard let go of nearly

New manager Oscar Stanage was a 1925 Christmas gift, according to Karl. K. Knecht. Evansville Courier & Press.

everyone from the 1925 team. A prominent businessman and the owner of Beard's Sporting Goods store in Evansville, Beard was also president and part owner of the team. He wanted more change. In early April, Beard declared the Pocketeers name dead. Another contest would decide a new team name.

On April 20, the new name was announced: the Hubs. Forty grandstand tickets were awarded to the winner, D.D. Martin. B.C. Burchler, of nearby Fulda, was awarded twenty grandstand tickets for his second-place submission, the Magnets.

Booms, Busts and One Global Disaster

Deadly Heat

The Hubs were half a game ahead of Peoria and one game in front of the visiting Springfield Senators to open a homestand on a muggy Saturday, July 3. The *Courier* reported a mercury reading of 100.4 degrees that afternoon. In the fifth inning, Springfield pitcher Jim Keenan faltered in the heat. A face familiar to Evansville fans, Ernest Regenold, replaced Keenan on the mound. Regenold had relieved Elmer Gray after hitting Louis Chedo the previous year.

Regenold blanked the Hubs in the fifth and sixth innings. At the end of the sixth, he told Springfield manager Alex McCarthy that he "felt fine." After giving up a triple and a sacrifice in the seventh, Regenold said he was feeling dizzy and sick to his stomach. He left the game and was attended to by Dr. William E. Barnes, who summoned an ambulance to St. Mary's Hospital. Barnes said Regenold had been having heart trouble for the last three weeks. Barnes termed the pitcher's problem "cardiac overstrain."

Springfield manager McCarthy and traveling secretary Ray Hamey sped to St. Mary's Hospital after the game to ask Regenold how he felt. A story in the *Daily Illinois State Journal*, a Springfield newspaper, reported that "as the hurler uttered the word 'better', he died." The hard-luck pitcher was the sole support of his widowed mother and younger sister at the time of his death. He was engaged to be married after the season. Officials said heart problems, exacerbated by the stifling heat, struck down the young hurler.

Regenold was transported via train to his hometown of Americus, Kansas, for burial. An estimated two thousand people attended his funeral. Ceremonies and moments of silence were observed before Three-I games on July 4.

Managerial Mayhem

The Hubs finished fifth in the Three-I, but only three and one-half games behind pennant-winning Springfield. Stanage was offered the job for the 1926 season and was given until November 1 to accept. The incumbent manager missed the November 1 deadline and accepted the position eight days late, telling Beard that he held off because "bigger fish" were in the water. Observers said the opportunity for an International League managership in Toronto fell through. Beard, in the meantime, had started

A view from the grandstands. *Courtesy of Willard Library Archives.*

a search for a new manager. He whittled the choice down to Terre Haute manager Roy Whitcraft, Punch Knoll and Stanage.

On November 14, Roy Whitcraft was selected as the new manager by the Fans Association Board of Directors. Beard would normally have made the choice himself but this time decided to place the three names before the board to decide. Whitcraft was a proven leader. His Terre Haute club had won the Three-I pennant in 1924, followed by second- and third-place finishes before Whitcraft accepted the Evansville job. He was known to be able to play any infield position if necessary. Evansville was set to "clean house," and his infield skills were a plus.

SYL SIMON: THE COMEBACK KID

A horrible accident stunned local diamond enthusiasts during the off-season. Sylvester "Syl" Simon was working his off-season job at Period Chair Company. He normally delivered tables, but on a busy Saturday, he helped with the mechanical saw for the first time. While maneuvering a piece of wood through the saw, it hit a knot and pulled his left hand into the sawblade. Simon was rushed to St. Mary's Hospital. Doctors were forced to amputate all but his thumb and "pinkie" finger in order to save his hand.

Syl Simon had a good year before the accident. He married the daughter of his first professional baseball manager in February. His bride, Thelma Knoll, was the daughter of Punch Knoll. He hit .308 playing third base for the Milwaukee Brewers of the American Association. The team won twenty-one games in a row during one stretch. His play put him on a trajectory back to the major leagues, where he had played briefly for the St. Louis Browns during the 1923 and 1924 seasons.

Simon received scores of letters expressing sympathy about his accident. One such letter came from Milwaukee Brewers owner Otto Borchert. It included a check for $100 and Simon's official release from the team. Simon wasn't ready to quit. Undaunted, he fashioned a special glove for his deformed hand. His bat had a steel attachment on the handle to slip his hand through for a better grip. He made sure that both glove and bat were within the rules. The bat and glove are now at the Baseball Hall of Fame in Cooperstown.

In the spring of 1927, Simon worked out with his father-in-law with the thought of becoming a pitcher using his good hand. He practiced with the Hubs as an infielder. Simon practiced so well that he made the club. On May 5, Whitcraft put him in the starting lineup at third base against Danville at Bosse Field. Syl beat out two infield hits and flied out twice to right field. He committed an error but had three assists in the field.

Simon appeared again at third in the first game of a road trip at Decatur. While sliding into second base, he injured the bad hand and left the game. He returned in July but was released after a ten-day trial. The Quincy Redbirds picked him up. Simon put together a solid year playing for Redbird manager and father-in-law Punch Knoll. Syl finished with a .279 average and 6 home runs. He hit .360 with 19 home runs for Fort Wayne (Central League) in 1928. He banged 30 homers the next year and hit .338 for Erie of the Central. Back in Fort Wayne for the 1930 season, he smacked 19 home runs with a .364 average. In his last full year, 1931, he hit .319 with Bloomington. Syl managed and played a little for Quincy in 1932 and ended a minor-league career with a .320 average and 1,259 hits. He had eight hits with the major-league Browns.

Punch Knoll retired from baseball after the 1930 season. He and Simon stayed in business as partners in Knoll's Orchard near Chandler, Indiana, until Knoll's death in 1960, when Syl turned to other jobs.

CHUCK KLEIN: SANDLOTTER TO SUPERSTAR

The Whitcraft year was abysmal. The club finished thirty-four games under .500. Whitcraft was let go. There were a couple of 1927 Hub bright spots.

A raw outfielder named Chuck Klein made a brief debut. The young fly-chaser batted .327 in fourteen games before breaking an ankle. He smashed his only two home runs in his second game at Peoria. Newspaper accounts of the game referred to Klein as "the sandlotter from Indianapolis." Klein's big game was overshadowed by other heroics. Hub shortstop Jess Runser pulled off the ultimate fielding gem, an unassisted triple play. With Tractor players on first and second, Runser snared a line drive, tagged the man running from first to second and calmly stepped on second base as that runner was nearing third. The Hubs needed every bit of the Klein and Rusner heroics to edge the Tractors, 8–7.

Klein attended Southport High School on Indianapolis's south side and was with the semipro Keystone Athletic Club when he was spotted by a probation officer from Evansville, Adolph Stahlman. Stahlman recommended Klein to Hubs owner A.G. Beard. Klein came to Evansville in August and was sold to Fort Wayne of the Central League in the off-season for $200.

For a short time, Evansville fans saw a future Hall-of-Famer. He went on to hit .331 with 26 home runs for Fort Wayne in 1928. Klein's manager in Fort Wayne was Punch Knoll. Chuck was called up to the Philadelphia Phillies in late summer and knocked 11 more out of the park (.360 BA). He never looked back after beginning a seventeen-year major-league journey that produced 300 home runs. Klein was posthumously elected to the Baseball Hall of Fame in 1980 by the Veterans Committee.

THE REICHERT GIANTS (1926–29): THE NEGRO SOUTHERN LEAGUE

Evansville's Louis Reichert Giants entered the Negro Southern League (NSL) in 1927. Team manager Charles Baker joined a strong circuit that first opened for play in 1920. For perspective, legendary pitcher Satchel Paige made his professional debut in 1926 with the NSL's Chattanooga White Sox.

The Reichert Giants played as an independent team around the Midwest through the 1920s. Another Evansville black independent team was the

Crescents. They merged with the Giants in 1925. Under their manager, Leroy Clemons, the Crescents played regularly against professional Negro National League teams in the early 1920s. The semipro Crescents played enormous schedules and claimed the "colored" championship of southern Indiana and western Kentucky in 1921. Other organized barnstorming and independent Negro teams in Evansville during the early part of the century were the Evansville Athletics (1909), the Evansville Maroons (1912) and the Evansville All Stars (1928).

Only the Reichert Giants achieved official Negro minor-league status. The *Pittsburgh Courier*, a leading black-owned newspaper, reported regularly on the Reichert Giants. In 1926, the paper called the Giants "the fastest club in the state" while covering the team's fortieth victory in its first forty-seven games. That season, the Giants defeated the Cleveland Hornets of the Negro National League, 1–0, in a thirteen-inning thriller.

A 1927 doubleheader showed Baker's team could throw and field. Facing the Evansville Eagles, Giants pitchers allowed just one hit during two shutouts wins. Giant hurler Raymond "Lanky" Austin, the team's ace, allowed a lone single in game one. Pitcher "Babe" Terry tossed a no-hitter in the nightcap.

The Crescents was a semipro team of the 1920s. *Courtesy of Willard Library Archives.*

The Eagles, an independent semipro team, were no slouches. They came into the twin bill on a twelve-game winning streak and had chalked up a win over the Class-B Evansville Hubs in an April exhibition game. After the double whitewashing, Reichert Giants fans were giddy. The *Courier* reported a female fan chanting as she left Bosse Field:

> *I'm so Glad,*
> *I'm about to Shout,*
> *The Reichert Giants,*
> *Shut the Eagles Out!*

The Reichert Giants got their name from Louis Reichert (who died in 1919) of the Reichert Construction Company. The elder Reichert left the firm to his son Manson. Manson Reichert was fanatical in his love for baseball, regardless of the skin color of those who played it. So passionate was Manson Reichert that he sanctioned the removal of his Giants from the field during a game against an all-white all-star team that included Punch Knoll. Manager Baker ushered his team out amid howls from a capacity crowd at Evansville's Eagles Park. Many attending maintained that the Giants were getting the "worst of breaks" from the officiating. The Giants led, 4–1, in the eighth inning when they exited, blaming poor "ball and strike" decisions.

Capacity crowds were commonplace for the Reichert Giants at Eagles Park, located at the corner of Weinbach and Washington Avenues. Charles "Dusty" Decker wrote of large crowds there during his tenure as sports editor for Evansville's black newspaper, the *Evansville Argus*. Decker recounted Sunday games with "stands crammed to capacity, the bleachers overrun and threatening to collapse at any moment, the large oak trees that overhung the fences were always filled long before game time." Decker was a combination shortstop and third baseman on the 1929 Reichert Giants and later served as manager of the Louisville Black Colonels in the U.S. League; the team played from the 1930s into the 1950s.

Decker recalled Manson Reichert's attempts to use Bosse Field, originally offering to play there only while the Three-I Hubs were away. Flatly denied use by the city, manager Charles Baker took a gamble and moved games to Eagles Park. Baker openly scheduled Reichert Giants games there while the Hubs were in town and playing at Bosse Field. Decker wrote that two to three thousand fans filled Eagles Park, while Bosse Field was "famished for patronage." Finally, agents of the Three-I League implored Baker to accept

BASEBALL

Bosse Field

HOPKINSVILLE, KY.

Vs.

REICHERT GIANTS

SUNDAY

(Double Header)

Game Called 2 O'Clock

MONDAY, TUESDAY

Games Called 3 P. M.

Hopkinsville is substituting for
Memphis because of accident to
members of Memphis team.

Above: Reichert Giant games at Eagles Field routinely outdrew the Hubs at Bosse Field. *Courtesy Willard Library Archives.*

Left: Hopkinsville filled in when seven Memphis players were injured in an automobile accident prior to a date with the Reichert Giants. *Author's collection.*

Bosse Field as the Giants' home, which he did. Eagles Park was condemned shortly after their move.

The other 1927 Negro Southern League teams were the Atlanta Black Crackers, Chattanooga Black Lookouts, Decatur (Alabama) Giants, Hopkinsville (Kentucky) Athletics, Jackson (Tennessee) Cubs, Memphis Giants and Nashville Elite Giants. Schedules were extremely flexible. The Reichert Giants' mid-June series with the Memphis Red Sox was replaced by a Bosse Field series against Hopkinsville due to an auto accident that injured seven Memphis players.

The circuit neared collapse early in the second half of the season, although a July 11 doubleheader sweep of Nashville drew 1,500 to Bosse Field. The *Courier* wrote that a Reichert Giants and Hopkinsville game was between "former members of the Southern Colored League" in August. The story said the league fell apart in July. The Chattanooga Black Lookouts were the 1927 Negro Southern League champions. The *Pittsburgh Courier* described the Reichert Giants as close contenders. Team records and statistics from the period are difficult to find.

The league lacked solid ownership and folded in 1928. Manager Baker still led the Reichert Giants through a strong schedule as sole owner of the club. Top teams in the south, like the Atlanta Grey Sox, Chattanooga Black Lookouts and Nashville Elite Giants, also continued to play independently.

The Negro Southern League was back in business for the 1929 season. Baker was voted vice-president of the league. The circuit was made up of six clubs: Nashville Elites, Evansville, Atlanta Grey Sox, Louisville Black Caps, Chattanooga Black Cats and New Orleans Black Pelicans.

The league faltered again and didn't finish 1929 with all of its original teams. Manson Reichert withdrew his support of the team because of reported political differences. Reichert served as mayor of Evansville from 1943 to 1948. The Giants were never the same after that and were defunct as a professional team by 1930. Nashville was considered the Southern League champs for 1929. Evansville's two one-year appearances in the NSL marked the only times, to that point, that a midwestern city was represented in this southern circuit. The Giants continued to play in the semipro circuits for many years.

COLEMAN COMETH

In the Three-I League, things were changing for the Pocket City. The 1928 Hubs negotiated the first working relationship with a big-league club: the Detroit Tigers. The move was an avenue to alleviate the constant churn of players from year to year and to minimize the amount of time needed to find players. The vague details of the agreement brought mild controversy. The Tigers gained control of the club, but questions surrounded who really owned the franchise.

Bob Coleman was named manager at the end of the 1927 season. Coleman told the *Courier* he alone owned the Hubs. Speculation was that the Tigers had financed the deal. The $20,000 to $30,000 price tag was too much for Coleman to afford on his own. Other reports said Coleman paid $10,000 for the team. Years later, *Courier* sports editor Dan Scism explained that the Tigers had purchased the team from the Fans Association at the end of 1927. G.A. Beard and the Fans Association ended their ownership interests and went about selling their assets. Players were assets, and this was a fire sale. Coleman began signing players once the transaction was completed.

Robert Hunter "Bob" Coleman was a strapping six-foot, two-inch former major-league catcher with Pittsburgh and Cleveland from 1913 to 1916 from Huntingburg, Indiana. He had managed here and there in the minor leagues since 1919, including a two-year stop at Terre Haute in the Three-

Eye. His 1922 Terre Haute team ran away with the pennant. He had just finished a year in Knoxville as manager in the South Atlantic League when he set foot in Evansville as manager.

Whitlow Wyatt

The 1928 Hubs improved under Coleman, finishing just six games under .500. The most notable addition to the club was a twenty-year-old Georgia pitching phenom named Whitlow Wyatt.

"Whit," as he was called, had been a high school football star at the fullback position who was recruited to play football at Georgia Tech. Tech offered Wyatt a football scholarship, and he wanted to go there, but the Detroit Tigers were so intent that their players abstain from the gridiron that they offered to pay his tuition on top of his new $3,000 contract to not handle the pigskin. Whitlow stayed a short time at Georgia Tech, ultimately preferring to start his professional baseball career in Evansville with the Hubs.

Wyatt began magnificently. In his first professional game, he struck out 10 and surrendered just 6 hits to the visiting Decatur Commodores in a 3–2 win. The *Courier*'s Dan Scism wrote that "for seven innings he sent his cannonball booming and a-whizzin' down the alley with such speed that the Commies were simply dumbfounded." The showing was enough for Scism to pen that the Hubs had a second Walter Johnson. Wyatt finished with a record of 14-12 in his first year as a professional.

First on Saturday and Third on Sunday

Next year, led by the overpowering pitching of Whit Wyatt, the 1929 Hubs played great baseball and led the Three-I by a game over Quincy with three games left in the season. Evansville was scheduled to play the last three games in Terre Haute.

A single game on Saturday ended in a heartbreaking 1–0 loss by the Hubs, but they still held fate in their own hands. A sweep of a season-ending Sunday doubleheader would give Evansville the Three-I pennant. One thousand Evansville fans traveled to Terre Haute on a special Chicago and Eastern Illinois train to see "the greatest finish in the Three-I League."

C.S. Smith, proprietor of Smitty's Grill in Evansville, ordered four hundred tickets alone, which were quickly snatched up by patrons.

Whitlow Wyatt took the mound for the first game. The teams battled into the bottom of the tenth inning tied at three when the Hubs' bubble burst. With one out, a routine grounder to the Evansville second baseman took a crazy hop over his head, allowing the Tots to score the winning run. Later that afternoon, the deflated Hubs lost, 3–0. It turned out to be a meaningless second game, because Quincy won its first game of a doubleheader against Springfield on the way to a sweep. The same day, Decatur swept Danville to grab second place.

"Hubs were first on Saturday and third on Sunday," was the lamenting line in Monday's *Courier* story. Wyatt had won 36 games in two years with Evansville.

Dazzling During the Depression

On October 23, 1929, the New York Stock Exchange crashed. Twenty-three leagues started the 1930 season, down from twenty-six the previous year. Two more leagues failed in 1930.

The Hubs improved with a first-place finish in 1930 but lost in the playoffs. The playoffs pitted the winner of the first half of the season (Danville) against the second-half champ (Evansville) using the Shaughnessy Playoffs System. This was the first of many playoff disappointments for Coleman. The 1930 team was one of the most talented and colorful clubs in the city's history.

The Hubs were stocked with pitchers. Thomas Jefferson Davis "Tommy" Bridges was as good as there was. Bridges pitched for Class-C Wheeling in 1929 and came to Evansville in 1930 throwing flames. He made national news on June 6 in a night game at Decatur when he fanned 19 batters in eight innings of a 5–2 Hub loss to the Commodores. The *Courier* declared it to be the world record for strikeouts by a losing pitcher.

Bridges mowed down 20 Springfield Senators on July 3 to set the all-time professional strikeout record. The previous nine-inning record was 19 strikeouts by Hugh Daily of the 1884 Boston Reds. Bridges managed 7 wins before being snatched away to Detroit before the season ended. His season strikeout record was remarkable. In 140 innings—twenty-eighth highest in the league—he struck out 189, which was first in the league.

A red-brick façade was part of 1930 renovations to Bosse Field. *Courtesy Willard Library Archives.*

Tommy amassed a career big-league record of 194-138 with the Tigers and struck out 1,674 batters. He appeared in four World Series for Detroit (1934, 1935, 1940 and 1945), with his last coming after service in World War II. His World Series record was a tidy 4 wins and 1 loss. As recently as 2014, he was still considered one of the top twenty Detroit Tigers of all time.

The Walker brothers, Harvey and Gerald, were "Hub" and "Gee" to Evansville baseball fans. Hub and Gee Walker had been teammates at Ole Miss. The brothers made up two-thirds of the Hub outfield and smacked the ball around the Three-I League at a torrid pace. The younger Gee hit .378. Hub hit .355 and scored 136 runs on 191 hits—both best in the league. Both debuted with the Detroit Tigers the next year.

Besides Bridges, the Hubs featured an eclectic and professionally prolific pitching staff. Johnny Niggeling led the staff with 19 wins. Niggeling, a knuckleballer, pitched nine years in the major leagues and won 64 games after reaching the highest level at age thirty-four with the Boston Bees. He was the winning pitcher in 223 professional games when combining his minor-league successes. Luke Daniel "Hot Potato" Hamlin was 18-7. Hamlin obtained his nickname due to his propensity to juggle the ball while getting ready to pitch. Hot Potato amassed 73 of his 286 professional pitching victories in the big leagues with Detroit and Brooklyn. The other

"Izzy" Goldstein and "Hot Potato" Hamlin were Depression-era pitchers for the Evansville Hubs. *Author's collection.*

213 came while laboring long and hard in the minors. Luke Hamlin was forty-five years old when he pitched his final minor-league game in 1950.

Third in pitching wins with 14 was Isidore "Izzy" Goldstein. Izzy was Jewish and one of only a handful of American ballplayers born in Russia. Goldstein's family had moved from Russia to the Bronx when Tsar Alexander III's "May Laws" began to threaten the growing Jewish population in the Ukraine.

ROB PETRIE?

Center fielder Robert Petrie joined the team in Danville, Illinois, and finished out the season batting .301 in forty-six games. The coincidence of a "Rob" Petrie joining the Hubs in the hometown of entertainer Dick Van Dyke was too interesting to ignore. Was this player the inspiration for the naming of the TV character? The question of Robert Petrie, the ballplayer, was presented to Vince Waldron, author of the definitive history of the show in his book *The* Dick Van Dyke Show *Book*.

"It's almost certainly a coincidence," said Waldron, who explained that the lead character's name likely came from Carl Reiner, the show's creator. The first name was likely from Reiner's son, Rob. "However, even if it is a coincidence, the fact that baseball's Rob Petrie also hailed from Danville, Illinois makes this discovery too delicious to leave unremarked," observed Waldron. "Am I the only one who imagines a five-year-old Dick Van Dyke attending his first minor league game in his hometown stadium and cheering as Rob Petrie takes the field? Who's to say it didn't happen?" Thanks to Vince Waldron for his imagination. Petrie quit the game after the 1931 season to go to work during the worst of the Depression.

The Hubs also signed twenty-one-year-old outfield Pete Fox. Pete was the fourth of six sons of Evansville Fire Department captain Henry Fox and a Bosse High School graduate. Since graduation, he had been working in a local furniture factory for a meager $18 per week. He kept his baseball skills sharp playing in the local industrial leagues and for semipro teams. Bob Coleman offered him $250 per month to play baseball for a living. Fox started so slowly that Coleman sent him to Class-C Wheeling after seven games, feeling he was too nervous to perform in front of the hometown fans.

A third-place finish in 1931 marked the end of the Hubs. Bob Coleman put a star-studded Evansville team on the field, headed by future Hall-of-Famer Hank Greenberg. Pete Fox was back. He batted .301 and stole 27 bases. Fox spent thirteen seasons in the American League with Detroit and Boston, appearing in three World Series. Pete Fox is a member of the Evansville Sports Hall of Fame and the Indiana Baseball Hall of Fame.

HAMMERIN' HANK GREENBERG

Hank Greenberg hit 331 major-league homers with a .313 lifetime average. In 1938, Greenberg entered the final game of the season as a Detroit Tiger with 58 home runs and a chance to tie Babe Ruth's record of 60. Hank went hitless in that game but became the first Jewish player to gain national notoriety in the sport. He is in the Baseball Hall of Fame.

Henry Benjamin Greenberg was always grateful to Evansville fans. Hank made lasting impressions on a few fans far beyond the .318 average and league-leading 41 doubles he rang up in 126 games for the Hubs.

Greenberg's teammates stayed at a rooming house operated by Minnie Lee Tipsword. Hank remembered Tipsword when he played in the 1934 World Series with Detroit against the St. Louis Cardinals. She was his guest at games in St. Louis and Detroit, all at his expense. Greenberg also credited the Tonnemacher family—John and Molly—as landlords when he lived with them at the rate of three dollars per week. The Tonnemachers had five of their seven children at home with them just a few blocks from Bosse Field. In a 1983 interview with Greenberg, then *Courier* sports editor Dave Johnson wrote that Greenberg treated the Tonnemachers to 1954 World Series tickets while he was a front-office executive for the Cleveland Indians.

LIGHTS UP AND LIGHTS OUT

The Detroit Tigers ended their affiliation with Evansville after four fiscally challenging years. The franchise was offered for sale at a price tag of $2,000 with no takers. Detroit's outdated rules contributed heavily to sparse attendance. Evansville was the only league team without lights. The stubborn Tiger brass didn't believe in night baseball and did not allow it until late in the season.

Temporary lighting augmented four light poles already used for football. *Courtesy of the University of Southern Indiana.*

Attendance rose dramatically when temporary lights were installed in August 1931. *Courtesy of the University of Southern Indiana.*

Bob Coleman gained approval from the school board to install temporary arc lights at Bosse Field for the final fourteen games. There were already four light poles that provided 60,000 watts for football games, but at least 150,000 additional watts were needed for baseball. The Giant Manufacturing Company of Council Bluffs, Iowa, was brought in to add temporary lighting to Bosse Field.

Hubs business manager Gil Ellis expected the largest crowd in history for the first night game on August 12, 1931. It drew only 3,041, but with lights, the club averaged 1,500 per game, a figure no team in the league could match. But it was too late. The damage was done. After a season-ending loss at Quincy, crews removed the lights. Observers speculated that things would have been much worse for the minor leagues without the inception of night baseball.

Halfway through the next season (1932), the entire Three-I League disbanded. By 1933, there were just fourteen leagues to open the minor-league season. The Three-I returned for the 1935 season, without Evansville.

4

BALL-FAKES, BEES AND BATTLES

1932–45

The In-Between Years

As political and economic pressures weighed heavily on the daily lives of Americans, Bosse Field remained a vibrant sports venue. Area schools used it for baseball, football and nearly any other activity that needed a large arena. A minor-league resurgence was seen between 1933 and 1940 as leagues grew from fourteen to forty.

Semipro leagues kept homes in Bosse Field. Servel, the Evansville refrigerator maker, was a strong sponsor of semipro baseball. Servel helped bring major-league baseball to Evansville during this period when it hosted the Cincinnati Reds for a Bosse Field exhibition game in September 1935

There was a close call in late May 1935 when efforts were made to move the Springfield, Illinois franchise of the reformed Three-I League to Evansville. Manson Reichert, part owner of the Springfield franchise, was not happy with home attendance. Bob Coleman co-owned the Springfield Senators team with Reichert. Springfield officials said they were prepared to open a homestand in Evansville on June 4 if all arrangements could be made, but there was too much to do with semipro and city softball committed to Bosse Field for the summer. The Three-I League folded again in 1936 but planned to open again in 1937.

JOE MATHES AND THE TEAM THAT NEVER WAS

On December 2, 1936, with little fanfare or warning, Joe Mathes was named manager of the new Evansville Hubs in the new Three-I League. Mathes was back from representing Manson Reichert and Evansville at a Three-I meeting. Team co-owner Reichert was told that his presence wasn't necessary. Mathes went alone and came back with a team. Reichert promised that lights would be installed in Bosse Field.

Mathes had major- and minor-league pedigrees that featured stints as a major-league second baseman with the Philadelphia Athletics and the Boston Braves. He spent 1914 with St. Louis in the Federal League and had managed, coached and scouted throughout the minor leagues since his playing days ended. In January 1937, the school board agreed to a rental fee of $1,500 per season for the field and agreed to refund up to $5,000 in rental to the baseball club over a five-year period for lights.

Early January was balmy with lots of rain in Evansville. Rain was followed by ice storms, more torrential rain and then heavy snow that quickly turned to slush. It was the wettest month in Evansville history. The Ohio topped out at nearly fifty-four feet and engulfed city streets. When the river crested and waters started to recede in early February, nearly four thousand Works Progress Administration (WPA) workers arrived to help put the soggy city back in order. Fortunately, none of the flooding reached Bosse Field. Mathes was away looking for players during the flood and, on returning, was pleased to see how well Evansville had recovered. Everything was clicking until March 1, when a newspaper headline shocked local baseball fans.

"Bloomington Is Readmitted to the Three-I" headlined the *Pantagraph*, the Bloomington, Illinois newspaper. League magnates named Bloomington, not Evansville, the sixth and final Three-I League member for 1937 at a meeting in Bloomington attended by Mathes. Most speculated that Mathes was in over his head. He and the city disagreed over the Bosse Field rental fee, and flooding caused so much financial hardship that league leaders thought Evansville might not support a team. Mathes couldn't afford new lights, and player contracts were adding up quickly. It was too much for him. Mathes never managed a professional team.

A Comic and a Cop-out

In July 1937, the *Courier* reported that the New York Giants were considering Evansville as a site for a farm club. Small-town baseball was getting back to normal with thirty-seven leagues in play. The Giants sent Frank Mackin to Evansville to compile a prospectus for Giant manager Bill Terry. Mackin touted Bosse Field after a visit with Mayor Bill Dress and *Courier* business manager A.G. Hollander, who had been working on the idea for three years with the help of Evansville native Joe Cook, a famed vaudeville and stage comedian.

Cook was born Joseph Lopez in Evansville in 1890. His parents died when he was three years old, and he moved in with foster parents. He took their last name. Joe was enthralled by the traveling tent shows that came to town. At fifteen, he moved to New York and took a juggling act to vaudeville. Cook's success in vaudeville led to a career in Broadway musicals, reviews and films. Joe became one of the top comedians and performers in the world. Evansville had a heavyweight in its corner.

Hollander and Cook invited Mayor Dress, Jerry Beeler and Colonel Louis Roberts to Cook's home in New York, where they met with Mackin. Beeler, an active civic leader, promised $4,000 to $5,000 in ticket sales before the season. Giant owner Horace Stoneham and manager Bill Terry shared interest. Terry knew Bosse Field from playing in a 1924 exhibition game there. Terry, destined for the Hall of Fame as a player, was in the process of leading the Giants to the World Series as manager. He had just signed a five-year contract at $40,000 per year to manage and oversee the farm system and needed a Class-B club.

Major- and minor-league officials attended the annual Minor League Winter Meetings in Milwaukee that December. Terry and other Giant representatives attended, along with leaders of core cities of the new Three-I League. Terry boldly stated that the Giants were ready to put a club in Evansville and asserted that they were "only interested in Evansville."

Less than a week later, hope was shattered. Terry and his Giants withdrew their offer.

COLEMAN TO THE RESCUE

"I'll get Evansville into the league if the boss says so," was Bob Coleman's rebuttal. His boss was Bob Quinn, president of the Boston Bees. Coleman was now with the Boston organization. The Bees were the old Boston Braves, renaming themselves from 1936 to 1940, hoping to change their losing image. The Bees were looking at minor-league cities.

A lighted field was the single demand made by Boston. Minor-league day games were played only on Saturdays and Sundays. Weekday game times catered to the workingman's or woman's schedule. A day after the first announcement, Boston paid two years' advance rental on Bosse Field, amounting to $3,000. It agreed to donate proceeds from one "Booster Day" game for the city to defray costs of new floodlights. The price tag for lights was estimated to be $7,000. Coleman said he'd arrange a second Booster Game, if that's what it took to get lights.

On January 16, 1938, Evansville was voted in as the eighth member of the Three-I League, now the oldest Class-B league in baseball. The league voted to conduct Shaughnessy playoffs to decide its champions at the end of the season. The system took the top four teams in the standings into an elimination tournament.

BEELER THE WHEELER DEALER

Civic leader Jerry Beeler was appointed chair of the Lighting Committee. When bids were in, they ranged from $15,000 to $22,000, so Jerry Beeler went to work to learn the lighting business from top to bottom in a very short time. Beeler went through five weeks of intense negotiations with the bidders and worked a miracle. Westinghouse won with a final bid of $10,654.12 and a promise to complete the work by May 1. The lights were tested on May 10, to the obvious pride of the town leaders.

The opener against Springfield was expected to draw as many as 9,000 fans. Unfortunately, rainy weather delayed the game by a day, and only 4,000 showed up. Undeterred, Beeler set about planning a second Booster Game. In late July, 6,345 turned out to help pay for the lighting. It was the largest crowd since Bosse Field's 1915 dedication. When the season ended, Beeler reported a surplus of $500 in his lighting fund.

BEES PLAY BALL

Mayor Bill Dress threw out the first pitch before 4,474 on Opening Day. The first Evansville Bees hitter, center fielder Jim McCarthy, knocked the first pitch out of the park for a home run. Harold C. "Hal" Manders, a right-handed fireballer fresh from the University of Iowa, took the mound for the Bees. Manders pitched well enough to win a 10–6 slugfest over the Cedar Rapids Raiders.

Manders was the cousin of another fireballer, future Baseball Hall of Fame inductee and fellow Iowan Bob Feller. Feller's and Manders's mothers were sisters. He won 14 games for the Bees. The hurler found more than baseball fortune in Evansville. In September 1939, he married Marabel Cross of Evansville. Manders spent parts of three years in the major leagues with Detroit and the Chicago Cubs.

The 1938 Bees won the Three-I League regular season by ten games over Decatur. A record 91,635 paid their way through the turnstiles, first in the league. The successful summer ended on a sour note in the

Opening ceremonies for Evansville's new team, the 1938 Bees. *Courtesy of Willard Library Archives.*

Above: Decatur Commodore players stand during Opening Day events, 1938. *Courtesy of Willard Library Archives.*

Left: Pitcher Hal Manders, Bob Feller's cousin and boyhood pal. *Author's collection.*

Shaughnessy playoffs. Third-place finisher Moline Plowboys dispatched the Bees in four games.

Coleman's crew featured another stellar pitcher. He was a twenty-eight-year-old rookie minor-leaguer named Floyd Giebell. The lanky right-hander was dazzling in his first professional year, winning 18 games and losing 4.

The Bees battled Cedar Rapids down to the last week of the season, only to fall a game back of the Raiders. The turnstiles turned to the tune of 81,371 paid admissions. That led the Three-Eye by almost 25,000 more than pennant-winning Cedar Rapids. Right-hander Joe Callahan paced the Three-I with 19 wins and was the ERA leader at 1.86. Outfielder Chet Ross was called up after the season after his team-leading 17 homers and .306 average.

Postseason woes continued. The Bees were ousted by eventual playoff winner Springfield in the first round of the Shaughnessy playoffs. The Browns of Springfield were fourth-place finishers during the regular season but took the championship from third-place Decatur.

STANDING (LEFT TO RIGHT) — MOHLER, FRYE, SCHOPPMEYER, CHENEY, GRIEGER, McCARTHY, HAZEL, RUCIDLO, MANDERS, GIEBELL, BOB COLEMAN, MGR.   KNEELING— HUBER, WIETELMANN, HODGIN, ZONTINI, HOUSE.   MASCOT— NORMAN FELLER.
EVANSVILLE BEE'S, INC.   OFFICIAL THREE I LEAGUE CHAMPIONS 1938

Three-I League regular-season champions of 1938. *Author's collection.*

A player is out at first in 1938 action. *Courtesy of Willard Library Archives.*

Manager Bob Coleman's 1939 Bees finished second in the Three-I League. *Courtesy of Willard Library Archives.*

For the first time, speculation about Coleman returning to Evansville was a topic of local concern. How long could he stay at the Class-B level after thirty years in organized baseball? Regardless, he and Mrs. (Albertina) Coleman publicly stated they'd make their permanent residence in Evansville. The next season would be his seventh managing in Evansville.

CATFISH AND MEATNOSE

In January 1940, baseball commissioner Kennesaw Mountain Landis issued what was referred to as the "emancipation proclamation." Judge Landis declared ninety-three Detroit Tiger players (eighty-eight minor-leaguers and five major-leaguers) free agents after a nine-month investigation of Detroit's mishandling of players and their alleged "coverup" of wholesale rules violations.

One "freed" player was a California-born Croatian, George Metkovich. The Boston Bees nabbed Metkovich and signed him for a sizeable bonus based on Casey Stengel's recommendation. Metkovich was optioned to Class-B Evansville for 1940 with a new nickname, Catfish, the result of a spring training fishing accident. Metkovich tore a ligament sliding into second base in June and spent much of the season on the sidelines, ending the year hitting .227 in only sixty games.

The E-Bees finished fourth in the eight-team Three-I in 1940 and drew 64,711 at home, best in the league. Infielder-outfielder Don Manno had a league-leading 113 runs batted in. Lee Hazel, a lefty, won 17 games for the Bees. Hazel played for the Bees every year of its existence from 1938 through 1942, winning 62 games.

Evansville Bosse High School grad, nineteen-year-old James "Lefty" Wallace, pitched four games for the Bees. Lefty later pitched parts of three seasons for the parent Boston Braves, with wartime service duty sandwiched between. Wallace was known later in life as a member of the Evansville Police Department. A former star athlete from Evansville Memorial High School, Donald "Jiggs" DeVault, spent half the season with the Bees. Jiggs later made his name as a radio personality for local stations WGBF and WJPS. He is remembered for his color broadcast of Evansville College (later University of Evansville) basketball games alongside local radio legends Marv Bates and Gus Banko.

The Bees exited in the first round of the playoffs. Cedar Rapids rolled through Springfield and then Decatur to back up its regular-season pennant with the league championship.

A fully healthy Catfish Metkovich returned in 1941, but the story of the year was about another southpaw. Warren Spahn came to Evansville after one year for the Bradford (Pennyslvania) Bees in the Class-D Pony League. During spring training in 1941, he ran into some bad luck and picked up a nickname, or two. A teammate's errant throw broke and permanently disfigured his nose. From then on, he was saddled with nicknames like "Hooks," the "Great Profile" and "Meatnose."

Spahn led the Three-I league in wins with 19, winning percentage (losing only 6), shutouts (7) and ERA (1.83). His 7 shutouts stand as the all-time Three-I League record; 3 were one-hitters. The Bees won the regular-season pennant easily with an 80-45 record. Metkovich played in 124 games and led the club with 30 doubles. Veteran hurler Lee Hazel won 11 games, including a no-hit gem against Decatur in August at Bosse Field.

Another league-leading season at the gate brought 69,156 paid through the Bosse Field gates, but the Bees were knocked out in the postseason's first round.

Baseball Takes a Back Seat

On December 7, 1941, the U.S. Naval Base at Pearl Harbor, Hawaii, was attacked by the Japanese. On December 8, the United States declared war. Baseball became secondary but still vitally important to the nation. After moving up to Class-A Hartford for the 1942 baseball season, Warren Spahn made a late-season appearance for Boston and then enlisted in the army.

Spahn fought in the Battle of the Bulge and was nicked by bullets on the abdomen and the back of his head. He was hit by shrapnel in another battle. When he finished his tour of duty, he was the most decorated ballplayer in World War II. His honors included a Purple Heart, a Bronze Star, a battlefield promotion and a Presidential Unit Citation.

Spahn was only the sixth player voted into the Baseball Hall of Fame on the first ballot, in 1973. Among his achievements are 363 wins and reaching 20 victories in thirteen different seasons. He could hit, too. Spahn's 35 home runs are the most ever by a National League pitcher, and his 363 hits matched his pitching wins.

STANDING (LEFT TO RIGHT) — BOB COLEMAN, MGR., DONOVAN, McELYEA, BROSKIE, GULLEDGE, SANDLOCK, CLEMENS, BURKHARDT, HAZEL, KILMER, CARR, BERNSEN, METKOVICH   KNEELING— DEFREITAS, SPAHN, HARRIS, FELLER-MASCOT, WOLF, McLAUGHLIN, SAGUTO
EVANSVILLE BEES, INC.

Warren Spahn (*kneeling, second from left*) was the star pitcher on the 1941 pennant-winning Bees. *Author's collection.*

Metkovich spent part of another season in Evansville, hitting .308 before moving to Class-A Hartford for the remainder of the season. He was reclassified 4-F and not eligible for military duty. In 1943, the Boston Red Sox offered $25,000 for his services. He spent four years there, highlighted by an appearance in the 1946 World Series against the Cardinals. In Game Seven, George hit a pinch-hit double and came home on Dom DiMaggio's double to tie the game. The next inning, Enos "Country" Slaughter of St. Louis scored from first base on a single when Boston shortstop Johnny Pesky "held the ball," giving the title to the Cardinals.

WAR STORIES

Forty-one minor leagues finished the 1941 season. Only thirty-one started in 1942. The Three-I persisted to completion despite the rugged travel, dwindling interest and, most important, the Selective Service. Government limits were placed on night games, particularly in coastal cities that had security concerns.

Coleman went into the first full year of World War II with plenty of new faces. Most minor-league clubs struggled to find quality players. This was an era of opportunity for some players and lost opportunity for others. Robert "Ducky" Detweiler was the Bees' new third baseman. He had started in pro ball a few years earlier in the Philadelphia Athletics organization and was traded to Boston's system in 1941. He was sent to Evansville for 1942 and went on a tear.

Detweiler hit safely in forty consecutive games beginning in June. His streak met its Waterloo on August 1 in Waterloo, Iowa. The Bees won the game, ignited by Bob Schmukal's long home run to center field. Detweiler's streak is still in minor-league baseball's top ten. Ducky ended the season batting .341 for the Bees and earned a September call-up to the parent Boston Braves, where he batted .318 in twelve games for manager Casey Stengel.

Detweiler was drafted into the armed services before the 1943 season and was transferred to Chemical Warfare Service Training at Camp Siebert in Alabama. There he helped the Camp Siebert Gashouse Gang become one of the most dominant military baseball teams in the southern states until the war ended in 1945. Detweiler played out his career in Class-B and D ball and managed minor-league teams for four years.

Robert C. Schmukal signed with the Boston Braves in September 1941. His athletic exploits were well known in the Buffalo, New York area. He played for the New York State American Legion champions in both 1939 and 1940 and was a star for his East High School teams in basketball, baseball and football. The six-foot, two-inch Schmukal finished high school and joined the Bees as a starting outfielder. He got off to a torrid start, hitting .350 after twenty-four games. As the season wore on, he slumped, ending the year at .230 in eighty-nine games.

Bob Schmukal entered the army in January 1943. His company landed at Normandy on D-Day. His company continued in the army's rapid charge across France. On October 3, 1944, Schmukal's jeep hit a land mine. Bob Schmukal was dead. He was buried at the Normandy Cemetery in Colleville-sur-Mer, France. The former Evansville Bee and Purple Heart winner was twenty years old.

THREE-I TAKES A BREAK

Distractions of war weighed on attendance and interest in 1942. A highly anticipated All-Star Game in Terre Haute flopped when only 2,300 attended in 16,000-seat Memorial Stadium. Cash receipts from the game fell significantly short of the $1,600 needed to fund the Three-I season championship and Shaughnessy winners' payout pools. First-place Cedar Rapids Raiders took the Bees out in the playoff's first round. The Madison Blues advanced to the finals over Springfield's Browns. The Raiders wiped out the Browns to take both the pennant and playoff titles. Attendance at Bosse Field slipped to 53,422.

Minor-league teams were struggling to put quality players on the field and paying customers in the seats. Many Class-B leagues disbanded before February 1943. On Valentine's Day, Three-I League president Tom Fairweather announced that his circuit would disband for the duration of the war. The league office remained open with the desire to start again after the war. Bob Coleman planned to work at Evansville's Chrysler Ordnance Plant. Evansville Bees players scattered to military service or to work in "war plants." Only nine leagues in sixty-two cities finished the 1943 season. Most teams were made up of players either too old or too young for military service or classified 4-F.

Two days after the league disbanded, Coleman accepted a coaching job with the Boston Braves. Bob Quinn, a close friend of Coleman's since his days as a minor-league catcher, was the president of the National League club. Quinn beckoned Bob to Boston to replace a departing coach. It was Coleman's second stint as a Boston Braves coach. The first was in 1926, when Quinn was also head of that club.

THE LIMESTONE LEAGUE

Joseph B. Eastman, head of the U.S. Office of Defense Transportation (ODT), held an emergency meeting with major-league team owners and Commissioner Landis in January 1943. The ODT was responsible for regulating transportation for personnel and goods during the war. The baseball group agreed to eliminate the normal practice of spring training in Florida and other warmer climates to save fuel and other expenses. For the duration of the war, baseball spring training would take place north of the

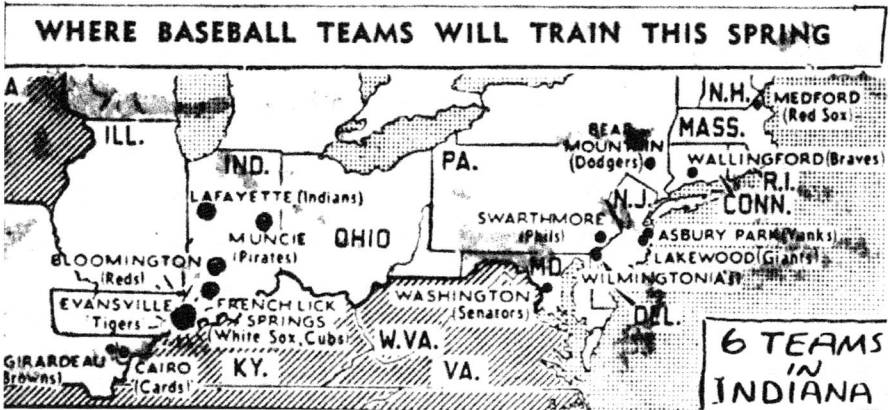

Karl K. Knecht's map of 1943 major-league spring training sites. Evansville Courier & Press.

Ohio River and east of the Mississippi River, except for the Cardinals and Browns of St. Louis. They could train close to home in Cape Girardeau, Missouri, and Cairo, Illinois. The eastern borders were north of the Potomac River and the Atlantic Ocean.

Six big-league teams chose Indiana for the new-look spring training. The Detroit Tigers picked Evansville and stayed at the Hotel McCurdy. The Cubs and White Sox settled in the small town of French Lick. The Reds and the Indians found homes on college campuses—Indiana and Purdue, respectively. Muncie was selected as the training home of the Pirates. White Sox players often warmed up in the French Lick Hotel ballrooms before facing the cool and damp Indiana spring. The White Sox moved training to Terre Haute for the spring of 1945.

Indiana towns unofficially made up the "Limestone League," named for the many limestone quarries in southern Indiana. Bosse Field hosted the first major-league games of the 1943 and 1944 seasons. The White Sox didn't have a suitable field when in French Lick, so they made the trip to Evansville to kick off the big-league baseball year. The first game of 1943 drew only 779 cash customers on Saturday. The next day, a crowd of 3,911 watched the Chicagoans win a thriller, 7–6. Men in the armed services were admitted for twenty-five cents on day two.

Springtime baseball moved back to the grapefruit and cactus states after the war.

Industry and Baseball:
The War Plant League

Wartime industry brought a high level of semipro baseball in a circuit called the "War Plant League." Team rosters were filled with talented players, many of whom had played professionally. Most players toiled in plants supporting the war effort. They played Tuesday and Thursday nights at Bosse Field with doubleheaders on Sundays. Bob Coleman had planned to manage a War Plant League team before he was summoned to Boston.

The 1943 version opened with six teams consisting of twenty players each, fifteen of whom could dress for games. Sponsoring teams were Servel, Republic, Chrysler, Sunbeam, the Shipyards and Camp Breckenridge (Kentucky). Teams were allowed only three members employed outside of the sponsoring organization.

Former E-Bees, like Russ Grieger and Lee Hazel, were All-Stars. Jiggs Devault of Servel led the league in hitting. An estimated 65,000 spectators paid to see games at a per-game ticket price of $0.25 for general admission or $0.50 for box seats. From the proceeds, $11,000 was divided among the teams. The Servel Wings won the first championship over Breckenridge.

War Plant League gate receipts were up by $7,000 in 1944. Six teams split $13,200 as nearly 53,000 fans paid to see games. Two exhibition games featuring War Plant League All-Star teams against the Boston Braves and Detroit Tigers helped the cause. Bob Coleman coached third base for the

War Plant League's Shipyard team. *Evansville Museum of Arts, History, and Science.*

The Metal Trades team in the 1944 War Plant League. *Evansville Museum of Arts, History, and Science.*

Braves versus the Don Ping–led All-Stars in front of nearly 3,500. The Tigers pulled out a 4–3 victory in front of 3,386. Punch Knoll returned to the sidelines as manager of the league All-Stars.

Teams from Servel, Republic, Metal Trades, Breckenridge, Jasper (the Reds) and the 820th Tank Destroyer Battalion played in 1944. Servel topped Breckenridge for the title a second straight year.

Eight teams started in 1945, but the war was over by midseason. Attendance slipped to thirty-three thousand, but players still split $5,000. The schedule was shortened to fourteen games. The final War Plant League consisted of Republic, Metal Trades, the Democrats, St. Phillips, Sunbeam, Chrysler, Sentry (Madisonville) and Meissner (Mount Carmel).

STENGEL'S REPLACEMENT

Coleman's coaching job with the Braves turned into a manager's position when his boss, Casey Stengel, broke a leg before the 1943 season. Coleman led Boston to twenty-one wins in the forty-six games that Stengel was on the mend. Coleman returned to his coaching duties but was again named skipper when Stengel resigned at the end of the 1943 season.

The Boston Braves finished sixth under Coleman in 1944, and he was retained as manager for 1945. Coleman resigned 93 games into the season amid Boston ownership changes. Coleman had two years left on a contract and remained as a scout. During his on-and-off three-year managerial career with the National League Braves, Coleman tacked up a 128-165 record.

Two dates in the year 1945, May 8 and August 15, brought the long, hard fights in Europe and the Pacific to their joyous conclusions.

REASSEMBLING THE TRI-ORB

Reassembling the Three-I League began almost simultaneously with the end of the war with Japan. Ramping back up was relatively easy. Tom Fairweather was a former mayor (Des Moines, 1918–19) and had terrific administrative skills. Fairweather scheduled a mid-September meeting in Springfield, Illinois, to discuss putting teams on the field in 1946. Nineteen cities in Illinois, Iowa, Indiana and Wisconsin planned to attend. An eight-team Three-I League emerged. Four were holdovers from the circuit when it had disbanded: Evansville, Springfield, Decatur and Waterloo. The "new" teams were Davenport, Quincy, Danville and Terre Haute.

Boston general manager John Quinn said Coleman would "run and manage" Evansville. Coleman was named president of the club by Boston-Indianapolis-Hartford Farm System Inc. Indianapolis and Hartford were the top two farm teams in the Boston system.

5

THE HOME OF THE BRAVES

1946–57

Baseball Is Back

The Evansville Braves were coming to town, as the parent club eschewed the Bees brand that Boston had used prior to the war. Opening Day drew 3,844 despite constantly rainy weather and rumors that the game wouldn't be played. The Braves were drubbed by Waterloo, 14–6.

Rain plagued the league during the first week, with few games dry enough to play. Evansville's next scheduled trip was to Waterloo, but because that town's ballpark was barely finished and underwater, the teams turned around and headed back to Evansville to play the series. The new Braves were mostly experienced minor-league players. Many hadn't played professionally since 1942. They scraped and scrapped their way to a third-place finish using players like Frank McElyea, a six-foot, six-inch, 220-pound first baseman from southern Illinois. McElyea had a cup of coffee with Boston in 1942 after playing for Evansville in 1941. This was his best professional year, hitting .316 with 10 homers. He quit professional baseball after the season to become an Evansville police officer.

The E-Braves locked up third place. On the last day of August, they beat Decatur in front of 8,057 paid, the largest crowd ever to see a baseball game in Evansville. It put Evansville over 100,000 for the first time in the city's professional baseball history. Third place got the Braves into the Shaughnessy playoffs, where history had recorded heartbreak and disappointment for

Baseball crowds are back for a night game in 1946. *Courtesy of Willard Library Archives.*

An overflow crowd for the return of baseball after World War II. *Courtesy of Willard Library Archives.*

Coleman and his teams. This time, the team got better, instead of worse, during the playoffs.

After a loss in the first playoff game at Davenport, the Braves ran off six wins. Coleman described it as "the best stretch of good baseball any of my teams ever had." The final three games were against Terre Haute. Coleman's crew left no doubt, crushing their rivals before a Terre Haute home crowd of 6,111 in the final game. The sturdiest Braves pitcher down the stretch, Bob Whitcher, was nearly flawless in the win. In a clubhouse meeting after the game, players and coaches voted to split the $800 winner's purse into nineteen equal shares.

At the final count, 117,045 paid to see the Braves play during the regular season, in addition to approximately 13,000 during playoff games. Those totals didn't include nearly 24,000 for Ladies' Nights. The entire minor-league system exploded with enthusiasm in 1946. More than 32 million fans went through turnstiles in forty-one leagues. The previous year's total attendance was less than 10 million with twelve leagues in operation.

The idea that nearly any town could support a minor-league team was supported by the fact that total attendance soared to over forty million per year in the years 1947 through 1949. Participation reached an apex of fifty-nine leagues in 438 cities and towns in 1949.

Johnny Logan

The E-Braves headed into 1947 with a full head of steam. Evansville teams had no shortage of players with Russian roots over the years. The new year added another one in twenty-one-year-old Johnny Logan, in his first stop as a professional. He lettered in football, basketball, baseball, golf and track, leading to his recruitment as a running back by gridiron powers Notre Dame, Syracuse and Colgate. Johnny stuck with baseball because of his diminutive size, weighing only 160 pounds.

After serving eighteen months in the military, with duty in Osaka, Japan, Johnny was honorably discharged. By then, the GI Bill had been instituted, so the youngster went to college for eighteen months at the Syracuse University extension in Endicott. That's where Bob Coleman offered Logan $2,500 to come and play shortstop in Evansville. Appearing in every Brave game, he batted .331 and fielded the position with flare and range that had never been witnessed in the southwestern Indiana town.

Anyone watching could see that this kid would not be in Evansville for very long. In fact, the next year, he went from Class-B to AA Dallas and ended the year at Boston's AAA affiliate in Milwaukee. Beginning in 1953, Johnny was the big-league Braves' starting shortstop for the remainder of the decade. The decade included two National League pennants with the Milwaukee Braves and a World Series title in 1957.

RAY FLETCHER: A NAME TO REMEMBER

With Logan, Evansville introduced a strapping outfielder named Ray Fletcher. He revisited Evansville many times in various capacities during his baseball life. His first encounter, in uniform, showed great promise. Fletcher had spent the previous year with the Owensboro (Kentucky) Oilers in the Kitty League. His year in Kentucky was so good that the Braves organization started him with its American Association (AAA) affiliate, Milwaukee, for spring training. The jump from Class-D to AAA was too fast, and he was dispatched to Evansville. Fletcher slammed 32 home runs, knocked in 120 runs and hit a sizzling .341 at Owensboro. His home run total ranks third for a single season in the defunct Kitty League.

Fletcher was impressive for the E-Braves, topping the Three-Eye in runs batted in with 115 on only 13 home runs. He was a run producer playing in a Bosse Field that was so big that a fair fly ball over the fences was rare. He so impressed the Chicago White Sox that they nabbed him in the minor-league draft after the season with the intention of turning him into a catcher.

THE COLLEGE GAME COMES BACK

Renewed enthusiasm for baseball extended to the college ranks. Evansville College resurrected a baseball program that had lain dormant since 1927. Basketball coach John Harmon pieced together a limited schedule of games from 1924 through 1926 for teams then nicknamed the "Pioneers" or "Rail-splitters." Opponents often used Kitty and Appalachian League players who had played collegiately until the spring semester ended. Most home games were at Eagles Field, where the Reichert Giants also played.

Another head basketball coach, Emerson Henke, brought baseball back in 1946 with a five-game schedule. Notable opponents were Camp Atterbury and the University of Louisville. Although it lost every game, the baseball program was back to stay.

The following year, Don Ping took over the baseball coaching spot he would not relinquish until after the 1966 season, when the school was renamed the University of Evansville. Ping was a catcher for Decatur, Terre Haute and Springfield in the Three-I League from 1923 to 1925 and coached in the War Plant League. His baseball teams used Bosse Field for important games. His Evansville fame first came as football coach at Evansville Reitz Memorial High School, where he won eight city championships and tied for two more. His teams won forty consecutive games at one point. He also served as Evansville College football coach from 1946 to 1954 and was voted "favorite professor" by the student body in 1963.

Don Ping is in the University of Evansville Athletic Hall of Fame and the Indiana Football Hall of Fame.

The college game still thrives in Evansville, with programs at the University of Evansville and the University of Southern Indiana.

THE GIRLS

The popularity of women's baseball was indisputable during the war years, as the All-American Girls Professional Baseball League flourished in the Midwest. The league is immortalized in an exhibit at the Baseball Hall of Fame in Cooperstown, New York, and in the movie *A League of Their Own*, in which major game scenes, including their World Series, were filmed in Bosse Field. The girls visited Bosse Field for exhibition games from 1946 to 1951. The league folded in 1954.

League tryouts were held in Bosse Field before two May 1946 charity games between the Grand Rapids Chicks and the South Bend Blue Sox. More than 4,000 fans attended the two games. In 1949, a "Courier Charities" contest between the Kenosha Comets and the Racine Belles drew over 1,800. The Comets beat the Belles, 6–2. Bosse Field was used as the home for the Racine Belles during the 1991 motion-picture filming. The film was released in July 1992.

HIGHLIGHTS OF 1947

Dick Manville was a tall right-hander in his first year of professional baseball after an Ivy League career at Yale and service in World War II. Pitching in front of 2,174 Bosse Field patrons, in his first game as an Evansville Brave, Manville tossed a seven-inning no-hitter against the Davenport Cubs in the first game of a July doubleheader. Seven-inning games were standard for minor-league doubleheaders. In his 6–0 win, Manville walked 3 and struck out only 1.

Another solid club went into the final week of the 1947 season with the talent to do damage in the Shaughnessy playoffs. In the second-to-last home game at Bosse Field, the Braves drubbed Danville, 12–0, with a Woods Drug Store Night crowd of 5,370 in the stands. That virtually clinched a playoff spot at three games ahead of fifth-place Waterloo with just three games to go. But a not-so-funny thing happened on the way to the postseason.

They dropped a heartbreaker in the last home game before a final doubleheader at Terre Haute. The Braves battled back all day, only to lose in the fourteenth inning on a bases-loaded walk with two outs. Future Brooklyn Dodger hurler and Indiana native Carl Erskine relieved for Danville in the bottom of the inning with one out. Erskine faced one batter, forcing a game-ending double play. That meant they needed to win one out of two at Terre Haute to clinch a playoff spot. A Three-I League record crowd of 10,600 witnessed the unimaginable. An Evansville team that had not been shut out in 125 consecutive games was whitewashed twice by the Phillies. The club's 70-55 record left them one-half game out of a playoff spot.

A new paid attendance record of 133,163 fans went through the Bosse Field turnstiles (more than 158,000 counting Ladies' Days). Waterloo set a Three-I League attendance record of 174,064 as the minor leagues continued to surge in popularity.

BOB BAGS BIG-LEAGUE BUCKS

How good was Bob Coleman? What was Bob Coleman's reputation in professional baseball? All you had to do was follow the money during the off season to find out. Cleveland Indians owner Bill Veeck Jr. wanted Coleman enough to offer him a three-year, $40,000 contract to join his organization. That is roughly $155,000 per year in today's dollars. Coleman's intent was to accept the offer and then tell the Braves organization. He didn't want to pressure Boston into raising his salary, but he couldn't stop the word from getting out. In no time, the Boston organization matched Veeck's offer.

"Cleveland does not have enough money to get Bob Coleman out of the Boston organization," said a relieved Boston Braves president Lou Perini shortly after Coleman re-signed. *The Sporting News* affirmed Coleman as the highest paid "official" in Class-B baseball. The ever-modest Coleman was "peeved" that things went down this way but was happy to stay home.

"I haven't too many baseball years left," Dan Scism quoted Coleman, now fifty-seven, as saying, "and I can't afford to overlook such a good proposition."

The Colored Braves and Evansville Dodgers: Hatten and McCray

Owners of the St. Louis Stars visited the city several times with visions of moving their faltering Negro American League franchise into Bosse Field in the early 1940s. The Stars' business and field manager, George Mitchell, visited the city five times and applied to the Evansville School Board for use of the field. Charles "Dusty" Decker wrote in the *Evansville Argus* that the applications were turned down.

Since the 1920s, Evansville had been without representation in the Negro minor leagues. The Evansville Dodgers and Colored Braves changed that. The teams were rivals mainly because their owners and operators were rivals. The Evansville Dodgers were first on the scene with a semipro club in 1948 and played established semipro teams. Team owner and business manager George McCray lived in Evansville. The Dodgers played home games at Bosse Field and Lincoln Field on the grounds of Lincoln High School. McCray's field manager was Rufus Hatten.

Hatten was twenty-seven years old with playing experience and lots of ambition. He grew up playing as a catcher in black semipro leagues in the Minneapolis–St. Paul area. He had short stints with the Chicago American Giants of the Negro American League (NAL) in 1944 and with the Negro National League's (NNL) Baltimore Elite Giants in 1946. Hatten also played for the baseball barnstorming Harlem Globetrotters in 1944. Hatten was catcher for the Asheville Blues of the Negro Southern League in the mid-to late 1940s and managed the Richmond Giants of the Negro American Association before appearing in Evansville in 1949.

In early 1949, McCray began a dialogue with Dr. R.B. Jackson, the president of the Negro Southern League (NSL), a minor-league organization based in Nashville. McCray wanted his Dodgers to make the step up to the minor-league level. By March, the chances of landing in the NSL looked promising for McCray, but the club was voted only an associate membership. The uncertainty of where to play home games made the league reluctant to grant full membership. Had Bosse Field been fully available, full membership likely would have been granted. McCray said the Dodgers would play most of their games on the road. McCray was elected first vice-president of the NSL and selected Rufus Hatten as player-manager for Evansville's first NSL franchise since the 1920s. President Dr. Jackson threw out the first ball at a Bosse Field matchup against the NSL's Nashville Cubs.

Hatten was unexpectedly released as field manager in early August after the Dodgers won twenty-six of forty-two under his leadership. Followers wondered why. McCray tabbed longtime area semipro player James "Big Jim" Bumpus as his new manager. The Kentucky-born Bumpus was a veteran of the Negro American League, having played for the Chicago American Giants in 1947 and 1948. Bumpus could also pitch. Hatten, curiously, continued to catch and play outfield for the Dodgers for the remainder of 1949. A Hatten versus McCray scenario began to emerge.

President R.B. Jackson announced in February 1950 that Hatten had been awarded the Dodgers franchise for the coming NSL season. Jackson said that McCray forfeited the franchise and "it was voted to Hatten." Hatten told the *Owensboro Inquirer*, "McCray is definitely out of Negro League baseball."

Hatten named his franchise the Owensboro Braves and said they'd play in Owensboro, Kentucky, and in Evansville. The team was referred to as the O-E Braves. Hatten planned to play one hundred games, splitting home games between Owensboro's Miller Field and Bosse Field. They also played games in Rockport, Indiana, and at Evansville's Lincoln Field. The Birmingham Black Barons visited for an April game at Rockport before Hatten's crew headed to Cairo, Illinois, for its Negro Southern League opener against the Atlanta Brown Crackers.

The O-E Braves' NSL home opener was on May 7 against the Nashville-Louisville Stars at Bosse Field, but on June 1, the Owensboro-Evansville Braves were dropped from the NSL for "failure to live up to contractual obligations." Hatten's Colored Braves played on independently. Rival McCray operated his Dodgers as a semipro club in the Illinois-Indiana

League. The Dodgers and Braves played several times during the season, with McCray's team playing at Bosse Field on days when the Evansville Braves were away on Three-I road trips. Other games were at Lincoln Stadium.

The 1950 off-season brought the rivalry between McCray and Hatten to a head. In late March 1951, the *Courier* quoted Evansville Colored Braves manager Rufus Hatten as saying his team would retain its membership in the Negro Southern League. On April 1, a *Courier* story stated that a local man, Leo S. Berry, had formed a partnership with Hatten and that both were attending a Negro Southern League meeting in Nashville.

The *Courier* covered the meeting and ran an unexpected headline, "Evansville Negro Nines Join to Enter Southern League." Dodger owners McCray and Jack Ramsey, and Colored Braves owners Hatten and Leo S. Berry, had purportedly cut a deal to merge. The two ownership interests agreed to enter the NSL with a team more competitive than either could be alone. Meetings were scheduled to take place after returning from Nashville, when the parties planned to "iron out all the angles" of the merger. Berry was elected NSL sergeant at arms. *Courier* sports department members gathered that all was "sweetness and light" between McCray and Hatten.

The merger meeting convened at Dodgers headquarters on Evansville's east side. The funny thing was that Hatten didn't show up. Without Hatten present, McCray was elected president of the Dodgers. Berry was named vice president and treasurer. Ramsey, a partner of McCray's, was picked as the team's general manager. Berry said that spring training would begin at Lamasco Field on Saturday, April 7.

On Monday, April 9, the *Courier* reported, "Hatten Revives Colored Braves." Hatten said he declined to join the merged clubs and instead would manage the Colored Braves in 1951. The team held its first practice that morning at Lincoln Field with a roster of nineteen players, according to Hatten. He announced that his Colored Braves would play the Chicago American Giants of the Negro American League at Bosse Field on May 4. Rufus Hatten had been working behind the scenes. Hatten said there was a chance for the Colored Braves to gain associate membership in the Negro American League.

Unfortunately, the Giant game was postponed by rain. During the rainout, Hatten completed a deal making the Evansville Colored Braves the top farm club of the Chicago American Giants. The deal came with perks. W.S. Welch, Chicago's manager, co-owned the American Giants with promoter Abe Saperstein. Saperstein was the widely known owner of the Harlem Globetrotters basketball team. Hatten's playing days with the Trotters' barnstorming baseball team in the 1940s helped put the alliance in place. Saperstein promised to furnish Hatten with a bus to transport the team from game to game. All Hatten had to do was travel to Chicago to pick up the vehicle. Hatten gladly obliged. Chicago could send players to Evansville under twenty-four-hour recall, and Colored Braves players could potentially make the big club. It appeared that Hatten had outmaneuvered McCray.

The Colored Braves' makeup game against the Chicago American Giants was a blowout. Hatten's team got drummed, 14–0. None of his players impressed Chicago management. Little was said about the working agreement after that, so the Colored Braves played a full schedule against all comers in 1951. It would be their last season. Hatten departed Evansville for other ventures.

McCray's Dodgers opened the 1951 season against the bearded House of David team at Bosse Field on May 15. The Dodgers played far and wide, including a trip to Canada where they won two games from the Port Arthur (Ontario) Giants. In March 1952, George McCray ceased operation of the Dodgers and moved to Pennsylvania to become general manager and part owner of the Pittsburgh Crawfords, a traveling Negro team. Affiliation of Evansville's all-black teams with professional organizations was over.

PLETHORA OF PITCHERS

Five pitchers won 10 or more games for the 1948 Braves. The hurlers averaged under twenty-two years of age as a group. Brave veteran Bob Whitcher, the elder statesman of the group at thirty-one, notched 14 wins with a team-leading 2.98 earned run average. The most intriguing hurler was six-foot, five-inch California right-hander Glenn Thompson. He lit up Three-I League batters with a league-high 220 strikeouts and the best winning percentage (15 wins and 4 losses). At nineteen years of age, Thompson looked like a future superstar. His problem was control. He led the league in hit batsmen and in wild pitches, and he walked more than six batters for every nine innings pitched. Wildness followed him throughout his professional career.

Dick Donovan had the right stuff in his second professional year. He came to Evansville after a tepid start in Class-C. Unlike Thompson, he regularly found the strike zone and walked only 50 batters in 187 innings

Bob Coleman (*back row, center*) poses for the 1949 Braves team photograph. *Courtesy of Willard Library Archives.*

while winning 12 games. He worked his way to the White Sox organization and appeared in the 1959 World Series against the Los Angeles Dodgers. Donavan finished his career with Washington and Cleveland, amassing 122 wins. The club finished third in the Three-I League regular season.

An eighteen-year-old outfielder drew most of the attention in the field. Dan Scism called the fly-chaser "the best-looking major league outfield prospect I've seen in many a year." Pete Whisenant from North Carolina became a fan favorite. He was unexpectedly solid at the plate, hitting .264 and swatting 8 home runs. He rose through the Boston minor league system, finally getting a shot with the big club in 1952. Pete spent parts of eight seasons in the big leagues with six different teams. He also played for the Cubs, Reds, Indians and Washington Senators/Minnesota Twins.

The Braves got hot in the Shaughnessy playoffs. They took down regular-season winner Quincy in the first round and then swept Terre Haute for the championship. The last win was in front of over 4,000 spectators at Terre Haute's Memorial Stadium. The victors took home $1,500 for winning the playoffs. Almost 102,000 fans went through the regular-season turnstiles, and nearly 16,000 watched the five home playoff games. The minors recorded its third straight record year, drawing almost 43 million.

DEL AND BUD

As the Braves began 1949 spring training, Evansville writers were touting two hot prospects: Del Crandall and Larry Pennell. Both were dispatched to the E-Braves from AAA Milwaukee Brewers of the American Association. Delmar "Del" Crandall was a catcher. Larry "Bud" Pennell played first base. Sam Levy, a veteran Milwaukee sportswriter, called these ballplayers "the best prospects the Brewers have had in 10 years."

Pennell attended Hollywood High School and was a baseball sensation. University of Southern California's legendary baseball coach Rod Dedeaux, an assistant at the time, recruited Pennell to play for the Trojans. After leading the Trojans in hitting as a freshman, Pennell signed with Boston. Pennell was nicknamed "Bud" by teammates and came to Evansville after hitting .338 in Class-D ball. He was twenty years old

Crandall, born in Ontario, Canada, was nineteen years old when spring camp broke. Crandall's family had moved to Fullerton, California, where both of his parents worked in the citrus-packing industry to make ends meet during the Depression. He started baseball on the sandlots and was chosen to be a catcher in elementary school. At Fullerton High School and summers playing American Legion, he was brought to the attention of scouts. Del's father didn't want him to sign with the Yankees, Dodgers or Cardinals, because they had too many prospects. Del turned down a $20,000 signing bonus from the Dodgers because the "bonus baby" rule would have required him to remain on the major-league roster for two years without minor-league experience.

Crandall signed with Boston for $4,000. He was one of the last players cut from the AAA Milwaukee Brewers. The organization assigned Crandall to Evansville to learn from Bob Coleman. "It was a break to work under him," said Crandall.

Neither Pennell nor Crandall were around Evansville long. Pennell struggled at the plate. He showed flashes of power (8 home runs in seventy-five games) but told some players that he was "going home" after going 1-7 in a July doubleheader at home. His teammates didn't take the threat from the fun-loving Pennell seriously. To their surprise, he took his .196 batting average and headed home to Hollywood the next day. Reports said Pennell had been bothered by dizzy spells after being hit in the head by a pitch during a game at Terre Haute.

Crandall left the club a month earlier than Pennell. It was white-hot hitting and superior catching that led to his quick departure. He hit a torrid .351

through thirty-eight games when the big Braves called him up on June 16 for a game against the Pittsburgh Pirates at Forbes Field. The president of the Boston Braves, Lou Perini, sent his private plane to Evansville to fly Crandall to Pittsburgh. Coleman called Crandall "the greatest catching prospect I've had in 27 years of managing clubs."

Boston planted Crandall firmly behind the plate from June 17 until the end of the season, making him the youngest starting catcher in baseball history. His major-league playing career lasted until 1966, when he played his final game as a Cleveland Indian. His first thirteen seasons were with the Braves in Boston and later in Milwaukee.

Coleman Called Up

Hitting woes worsened without Crandall. Coleman depended on a solid group of young pitchers. Leading the mound crew was Chester "Chet" Nichols Jr., a left-hander. Chet was only eighteen years old but won 14 games (2.32 ERA) in his first professional year. He later pitched with the Boston Braves, Milwaukee, Boston Red Sox and Cincinnati and went 34-36 at the highest level over nine seasons.

Righty David Sheehan was in his last professional baseball stop after bouncing around the minors since 1944. He tallied 15 wins (2.38 ERA). Clarence Peters chipped in with 13 wins and a nifty 2.82 ERA. The E-Braves pitching staff allowed only 963 hits in 1,107 innings pitched. Coleman's team was last in the Three-I in hitting and seventh in fielding but won thirty-five games by a single run to capture the regular-season pennant by four and a half games. A record 145,657 poured through the gates. Players split $2,000 for their regular-season pennant.

Evansville took down the rival Terre Haute Phillies in the first Shaunghessy series, but the final game came at a cost. Pete Whisenant separated a shoulder diving for a fly and was out for the season. Charles Samson, another regular outfielder, was out with an injury. Pitcher Joe Reardon started in center field in the championship series against the Davenport Pirates but suffered a freak accident. He was sidelined when he fell on a bottle and slashed his throwing arm playing with some kids outside of Bosse Field. Catcher Gene Edwards was forced to the outfield. The tattered and battered Braves ran out of players and gas. Davenport swept the series and grabbed the $1,500 winner's check. The Braves split $1,000 as runner-up.

A few days before Thanksgiving, Bob Coleman signed a two-year contract to manage the AAA Milwaukee Brewers, Boston's top minor-league affiliate in the American Association. There, he was reacquainted with several of his former Evansville players, including Johnny Logan and Pete Whisenant. "Evansville is such a fine baseball town that I naturally regret leaving," he told the *Courier*. "This [Evansville] is my home, and this is where I want to live." He and Mrs. Coleman stayed in their home on South Alvord Street.

A thirty-three-year-old former major-league pitcher and recent Boston Braves coach, Ernie White, was named the new pilot of the E-Braves. He was introduced by Bob Coleman. "I'm still president of the Evansville Club," explained Coleman. White was young but had a major-league pedigree and spent a season as a minor-league manager at Bluefield (West Virginia). His major-league resume included a 17-7 record in his first full year with the St. Louis Cardinals in 1941. In 1942, he tossed a shutout at the New York Yankees before the largest World Series crowd in history. He signed with Boston after the war.

RALPH BEARD: ALL-AMERICAN BRAVE

The biggest name on the 1950 Braves roster came with the caveat that he would miss much of spring training because of another sport. Ralph Beard was in his first season as player-owner of the NBA's Indianapolis Olympians and was considered a long shot to make the club. Beard and the University of Kentucky had won the 1948 NCAA title over Baylor at Madison Square Garden. Beard helped win Olympic gold for the United States at the 1948 London games.

He joined the Braves for their first Bosse Field exhibition game on April 15 against Evansville College. Another former basketball star and E-Braves player, Frank Schwitz, was college coach Don Ping's left fielder that afternoon. Schwitz appeared in a few games with the E-Braves as a relief pitcher right out of high school in 1946. His Evansville Central High School team went to the state finals in Indianapolis a couple of months before Bob Coleman signed him. Schwitz returned to college to play both baseball and basketball after a couple of years in the minors.

Beard made the club as second baseman, edging out African American George Handy. He suffered injuries, the flu and was knocked unconscious from his own bat when a ball he fouled off sent the bat into his noggin. Ralph batted .247 and tied for the team lead in triples with 7. He got into ninety-eight games and was the fans' favorite.

With a pitching staff ranging in age from eighteen to twenty-one, the team stumbled to a 56-70 final record, missing the playoffs for the first time since 1947. The weak-hitting team hit 35 long balls during the 126-game season. The best game by a pitcher was turned in by manager Ernie White on September 4. With little to play for, manager White put himself on the mound for the first game of a doubleheader. He pitched a complete game five-hitter, winning 5–1. The club tallied 102,865 paid customers. The Terre Haute Phillies won the regular-season pennant and dominated in the Shaughnessy playoffs.

BOB IS BACK

Bob Coleman's first year in Milwaukee resembled White's in Evansville. The talent wasn't Class-AAA level, and the Brewers limped in with a 68-85 record. Attendance was a mediocre 145,000. The downward attendance trends were not attributed solely to the mediocre performance of either team. Generally, entertainment and comfort options were expanding at a rapid pace. There were more and more choices. Minor-league baseball's postwar honeymoon was ending. Although fifty-eight leagues were in operation, total minor-league attendance dropped by a staggering seven million to just under thirty-five million.

Despite the off years, Coleman and Ernie White expected to remain in their jobs for the 1951 season—until late September, when president of the Milwaukee club, D'Arcy "Jake" Flowers, announced his resignation. Rumors circulated that Coleman would return to Evansville and former White Sox player Jack Onslow would get the Milwaukee managership. Boston general manager John Quinn confirmed that Bob Coleman was heading back to Evansville as president and field manager of the Evansville Braves. White ended up as manager of the Cincinnati Reds' Class-A affiliate in Charleston, West Virginia.

KOREAN CONFLICT

On June 25, war broke out on the Thirty-Eighth Parallel as North Korea moved toward Seoul, South Korea. President Harry S. Truman committed American forces to a combined UN effort. The Selective Service draft had been reintroduced in 1948 because of the Cold War, immediately affecting baseball.

Former E-Brave Larry Pennell was ready to continue baseball but was drawn to the fight. Bud served in counterintelligence in the U.S. Army from 1950 until 1953. Fan favorite Ralph Beard told the *Courier* he didn't plan to play baseball and remained in Indianapolis to play for the Olympians.

Minor-league baseball lost eight leagues over the winter and was down to fifty. The Three-I loop had a new president and two fewer teams. Vern McMillan, a former Terre Haute mayor, took the reins from Tom Fairweather. Fairweather retired at the end of the 1950 season and sadly passed away in January 1951 at the age of seventy-one.

Six Three-I teams played each league member twenty-six times—thirteen at home and thirteen on the road. The E-Braves were a little more mature than the fuzzy-faced teams of the past few years. Veteran minor-leaguers like outfielder Duri "Lucky" Vital, at twenty-four, helped stabilize the club. Future major-league pitcher Ben Johnson played for the Braves in 1949 and returned after a year with Coleman in Milwaukee. Ray Fletcher was behind the plate after notifying the Boston brass that Evansville was the only team he would play for. Now an Evansville resident, Fletcher wanted to be at home in uniform or just plain home. The best pitcher was a twenty-six-year-old professional baseball rookie from Windsor, Canada, named Alfred Dumouchelle. The Canadian won 17 games with a nifty 2.49 ERA. Nineteen-year-old lefty Jack Lutz chipped in with 16 wins. A twenty-year-old fly-chaser from the Ohio State University, Jim Frey, was a pleasant surprise. He led the team in batting (.324) and slugging percentage (.425).

THE GOLDEN YEAR

The year 1951 marked the golden anniversary of the Three-I League. Local sportscaster and radio voice of the Braves Dick Shively served as master of ceremonies for Opening Day at Bosse Field to begin the circuit's fiftieth year.

Mayor Ed Diekmann welcomed back the old master. "I'm certainly glad to be back home," said Coleman during the pregame ceremony.

The weak-hitting team was the victim of a no-hit game around midseason. It was tossed by a tall right-hander from Hollywood, California. Six-foot, four-inch Quincy Gems pitcher Dick Fiedler stymied the Braves at Bosse Field on July 2. At shortstop for the Gems was a feisty New Yorker, George Noga. He would refamiliarize himself with Evansville and Bosse Field in a nonplaying role fifteen years later.

The club finished second to the Terre Haute Phillies with a 69-60 season mark and league-leading attendance of 101,254. Overall, minor-league attendance dropped 20 percent. The Cedar Rapids Indians took out the E-Braves in the first round of the Shaughnessy playoffs. Quincy downed Terre Haute and Cedar Rapids for the playoff crown. Shortly after the Three-I season, it was announced that the Iowa towns of Keokuk and Burlington would be added for the 1952 slate. They put down $1,000 each to join. Keokuk was nicknamed the Kernels, and Burlington went with the Flints.

BEARD'S BLUNDER

The off-season was rocked with news that Braves alumnus Ralph Beard was implicated in the collegiate basketball point-shaving scandal. After months of investigation, Alex Groza and Beard were nabbed after a college basketball All-Star Game at Chicago Stadium on October 19. The two were accused of accepting bribes to shave points in a 1949 NIT game at Madison Square Garden. Loyola of Chicago beat Kentucky by eleven points in what the Associated Press called "an amazing upset."

"It's like a load's been lifted," said Beard after the arrest. "I couldn't walk down the street without feeling someone was following me." He never denied taking money but forever maintained he did not shave points. Those who knew Beard believed that to be true. The players were convicted the following year, and their sentences were suspended. National Basketball Association president Maurice Podoloff banned Beard and Groza from the NBA for life. Beard's requests to return to professional baseball were also denied. The lone victory for Beard and Groza was affirmation from U.S. Olympic Association president Avery Brundage that they could keep their 1948 gold medals.

Beard received $700 from the gamblers. He claimed that he never did anything untoward in a game. "I took it [the bribe] because I had no money. None," explained Beard.

GARNER AND MANTILLA

A new Three-I League president was elected in November. The new leader in 1952 was a well-known radio broadcaster. Hal Totten was the first to call an entire slate of home games for a major-league team. He did so for the Chicago Cubs in 1924 on WMAQ. He was behind the microphone for Babe Ruth's "called shot" in the 1932 Series.

After two listless years at the plate, the Braves topped the league in hitting behind two newcomers: outfielder Horace Garner and shortstop Felix Mantilla. Garner was an older pro with professional baseball beginnings in the Negro Leagues. Mantilla was seventeen years old. Together, they broke the color barrier in Evansville minor-league baseball.

Garner was twenty-seven years old when he came to Evansville. Born in St. Louis, he started his professional career in 1949 with the Indianapolis Clowns. In June of that year, he moved to play for the Kansas City Stars. The next year, Garner played semipro ball in McCook, Nebraska, where he was signed by a scout for the Boston Braves. Mantilla was Puerto Rican and fresh from playing on the winning World Amateur Baseball Championship team with his home country in 1951. Garner was the league's Most Valuable Player. Mantilla garnered the Most Outstanding Rookie award.

Garner hit .318, slugged 23 home runs and drove in 107. Mantilla batted .323. Slugging third baseman Joseph Andrews (.311 BA, 15 HR) and returning outfielder Jim Frey (.336 BA) added to the firepower. A solid pitching staff had the Braves cruising to an almost insurmountable eight-and-a-half-game lead over Terre Haute as the season went down the home stretch.

The Terre Haute Phillies won twenty of their last twenty-two games and pulled within a half game of Evansville with a season-ending doubleheader remaining against the Braves on the Phillies' home field. Karma may have been on Bob Coleman's side on this Labor Day. It rained. And it rained. And it rained. The Terre Haute grounds crew worked feverishly all day to fix the Municipal Stadium field. When it looked like the field might be

Felix Mantilla (*kneeling, second from left*) and Horace Garner (*top row, far right*) broke the color barrier with the 1952 Evansville Braves. *Courtesy Willard Library Archives.*

ready for the scheduled 7:30 p.m. start time, a late-afternoon cloudburst turned the playing surface into a quagmire. At 3:30 p.m., Coleman told reporters he'd rather give Terre Haute the pennant than risk players injuring themselves. League president Totten agreed and canceled both games. With no makeup dates available, Evansville was awarded the pennant by one-half game over the Phillies. Braves players split the purse of $2,000.

The E-Braves won the opening series over Burlington, but bad luck struck in the deciding victory at Burlington. Mantilla was carried from the field late in the game with a badly twisted ankle. Evansville opened the championship series against Terre Haute to an overflow Bosse Field crowd of 5,387 but without Mantilla. Terre Haute won three of four, exacting some revenge for the weather-related regular-season loss. The Phillies received $1,250 for winning. Evansville players got $750 to split for second.

Evansville Braves 1952 program and scorecard. *Author's collection.*

TELEVISION AND TEAM MOVES

Evansville drew 124,381 in 1952, more than 20,000 above the previous year. The wildly successful 1952 Terre Haute team drew only 62,000. The attendance pullback was true for most Three-I teams. The conflict in Korea didn't help matters from a talent standpoint. Around 2,500 NAPBL players were in military uniform. Entertainment and comfort technologies hurt as well. Evansville Braves business manager Lynn Stone talked to the *Courier* about the influence of TV.

"It will be the same story here as in Terre Haute, California, and others. Attendance will drop when a TV station operates here, and the snow disappears from the programs," stated Stone. Stone was referring to the snowy look of broadcasts pulled in on television antennas from faraway stations. Terre Haute was getting strong reception from stations in Indianapolis and Bloomington.

Evansville's parent team was struggling. Boston Braves president and controlling stockholder Lou Perini reported the largest operational loss ever experienced by any team in the history of baseball. On March 18, 1953, Perini announced that they were moving the team to Milwaukee in time to open the season. National League owners unanimously approved.

Thirty-nine leagues began the 1953 season, down twenty from the zenith after World War II. A U.S. senator from Colorado acted to do something about it. Democrat Edwin Johnson introduced a bill that would leave it up to individual teams whether to allow major-league broadcasts in minor-league towns. Johnson claimed that broadcasts, many now on television, were destroying minor-league baseball. His bill did not pass.

The 1953 club finished in third place and earned $750. The Terre Haute Phillies won the regular-season pennant and were dispatched by Evansville in the first round of the playoffs. The Braves were then taken down by Quincy, led by their wunderkind first baseman Marv Throneberry. He hit 30 home runs to lead the Three-Eye. Brave attendance fell to 88,438. The minors were down to thirty-eight leagues and witnessed nine cities either move or withdraw during the season. The parent Braves went last to first in baseball attendance, drawing over 1.8 million fans to County Stadium. That set a National League season record.

The year was a masterful managing job by Coleman. A couple of future big-league hurlers—Don McMahon and Humberto Robinson—led the way. Robinson topped the club with 17 wins. Power-hitting second baseman Leonard "Preacher" Williams jacked out a modern club record 24 home

Preacher
Williams and
Humberto
Robinson of the
1953 Braves.
*Courtesy Willard
Library Archives.*

runs. Future major-leaguer Wes Covington showed promise before he was drafted into the army. Outfielder Johnny Turco led the club with a .332 average, and Bud Pennell was back for another try after three years in Korea.

MR. HOLLYWOOD

Larry "Bud" Pennell's season hinted that he might be a major-league talent. He swatted 16 homers and 11 triples. He averaged .276 and showed that he could play outfield and first base. When the satisfying season ended, Pennell headed for his western home turf. This time, the path home didn't take him directly to Hollywood. He detoured through Las Vegas and spawned the *Courier* headline "Bud Pennell Elopes with Starlet." A picture of the handsome ballplayer in his Evansville Braves baseball cap accompanied the story of newlyweds Larry Pennell and Pam Gallagher.

They were honeymooning in Hollywood after a surprise elopement hours after he arrived in Vegas from Evansville.

Pennell signed a Paramount Studios contract for 1954. His baseball playing days were over. He said he still loved baseball but that the money was better in movies. Pennell said he had one regret about giving up his baseball career. "Although my Dad doesn't say it, I know it really hit him. He goes to the movies once every three years but reads the sports pages every day. He can tell you what Ty Cobb hit in 1914," said Pennell.

The Hollywood thing worked out. Bud Pennell tallied more than four hundred credits across stage, film and television during his acting career. He may be best remembered for his campy portrayal of Dash Riprock in the television series *The Beverly Hillbillies*. His career came full circle in 1992, when he appeared as baseball scout Howie Gold in *Mr. Baseball*, a film starring Tom Selleck. Selleck implored Pennell to take a part in the movie about a washed-up major-league player relegated to playing in Japan. As Howie Gold, Pennell was in Japan to scout Jack Elliot, the Selleck character. Pennell's last film appearance was in 2011.

Legendary sportswriter Furman Bisher lamented Pennell's passing as a baseball player in a 1959 *Saturday Evening Post* article: "His [Pennell's] future seemed unlimited. I shall always be frustrated by a desire to know how great a star he might have become."

WEHT and WFIE: TV Timeout

The Ohio Valley Television Corporation declared that broadcasting to the tri-state area would begin on September 27, using UHF channel 50. The TV tower was physically located in Henderson. The station used the call letters WEHT, standing for "Watch Evansville Henderson Television." Meanwhile, WFIE announced it expected to be on the air a little more than a week later with test patterns on channel 62 from a tower in Evansville. The introduction of local television stations was a boon to appliance and TV stores. A spokesman for locally owned retail store Kirby Sales said its 400 percent increase in sales meant it had to add several men to handle installations. The impact of local television stations on baseball in Evansville was yet to be determined. The season provided some answers. Thirty-six minor leagues started the 1954 season. Thirty-three survived the season.

After a fast start to the season, the E-Braves lost nine straight games and fifteen of sixteen and sat in fifth place. After breaking the losing streak with a win over Terre Haute, the club stood at 35-34 and in fifth place. Following the losing skid, the club won forty-seven of its final sixty-seven games to claim the Three-I pennant. Pitcher Ray Ripplemeyer won 13 consecutive regular-season games to close out the year. Newcomer and former Duke University standout Al Spangler showed up after college and added a spark to the outfield. It was Spangler's first year in a professional baseball career that ended in 1971 after thirteen big-league seasons.

The E-Braves ran out of gas in the playoffs. Third-place Peoria took Evansville out in the first round. Quincy rolled over Peoria for the Shaughnessy playoff trophy. Keokuk featured a young outfielder named Roger Maras, who spanked 32 home runs. Somewhere between the 1954 and 1955 seasons, the shy and sensitive youngster changed his last name, hoping to avoid taunts of opposing fans who had taken to shouting "Mare-Ass." Playing for Reading (Pennsylvania) the next season, "Maris" appeared in box scores and stayed that way.

The E-Braves banked the $2,000 winner's check for the league title, but only 71,691 fans went through the turnstiles. All league clubs reported losses; only Evansville, Waterloo and Cedar Rapids looked healthy enough to continue. Despite the rose-colored glasses, 1955 didn't start well.

The club was tracking toward less than 60,000 in attendance for 1955. Coleman needed 100,000 to break even on expenses. The local on-field product was losing to new television stations providing crystal-clear, black-and-white broadcasts. Future major-leaguers filled league stat sheets. Russ Nixon led the circuit in hitting for Keokuk. Future Yankee shortstop and later *Baseball Game of the Week* television commentator Tony Kubek of Quincy was first in hits. Waterloo catcher John Romano set a Three-I League record for home runs in a season with 38. The slugging catcher broke the longtime mark of 36 established by Evansville catcher Frank "Germany" Roth in 1901. Keokuk was the most dominant team in Three-I history, winning ninety-two games and losing thirty-four. The Braves finished six games under .500 in fifth place and missed the playoffs.

LEE MAYE: A DOO-WOP DANDY

A young outfielder from Los Angeles debuted in Evansville. Like Bud Pennell, he had other talents. Lee Maye—or Arthur Lee Maye, as he appeared on record labels—was a singer, and a very good one at that.

Jack Burns (*1B*), Roger Jongewaard, Bill Rittman (*3B*), Joe Unfried (*LF*), Lee Maye (*RF*), John Stratton (*2B*), Billy Smith (*CF*) and Bill Thomas (*SS*) of the 1956 Three-I League champs. *Courtesy Willard Library Archives.*

On Maye's arrival at spring training, his teammates began calling him "Willie" Maye, because he flashed athletic talents like a rising big-league star of the day. Maye also answered to "Art" but preferred "Lee" for baseball and "Arthur Lee" for his singing career. He sent off for some of his records from back home to prove to his new mates that he was a recording artist. Maye recorded his first record as part of a trio in February 1954 before reporting to Boise for his first assignment with the Braves organization. The Flair Records label named the trio the 5 Hearts and released the single "The Fine"/"Please Please Baby." After his first year in baseball, Lee formed a group known as the Crowns. Doo-wop was its style.

Maye spent May with the Braves before he was sent down for more seasoning, spending most of the season with Yakima (Washington) of the Northwest League.

JOE UNFRIED: HOME COOKING

Coleman needed some offensive firepower. Hometown boy Joe Unfried had decided he wouldn't play professional baseball in 1955, until he got a phone call from business manager Lynn Stone. Unfried starred in several sports at both Memorial High School and Evansville College. He chose not to report to Class-C Albuquerque in 1955. With a little girl just over two years old, his wife, Lois, had seen enough of life on the road. She called Joe and said, "I want you to come and take me home."

Unfried had a great year at Class-A Wenatchee (Washington) in 1954 and finished the year in AAA at Oakland. The assignment to Class-C didn't sit well. "It's no picnic for me either," was Joe's reply to Lois's telephoned request. They packed up and headed home to Evansville. It took a little doing to get him out from under his Albuquerque contract. First, Oakland had to recall him. They did and sold him to Evansville.

Unfried was known in southern Indiana sports circles. After playing for powerful Memorial High School football teams, he joined former Memorial football coach Don Ping at Evansville College. Unfried left college in 1949 to play minor-league baseball for two years, first with Class-C Stockton (California) and the next season up a level in Wenatchee. There, he played every day and hit .303. Then he came home expecting a call from Uncle Sam. It didn't come right away, so he continued to work on his college degree.

Unfried got the call in August 1951 and was assigned to Camp Breckenridge (Kentucky). He played baseball and football for the camp team until August 1953. Joe played in the 1951 Refrigerator Bowl as the camp's punter and second-string fullback. The Refrigerator Bowl was played annually from 1948 to 1956 in Evansville's Reitz Bowl. Unfried is the only player to appear in three Refrigerator Bowl games. He was part of winning teams at Evansville College in 1948 and 1949. After a playing career, Unfried was the Bosse High School baseball coach in the mid-1980s. He also taught, headed the physical education department and served in athletics management roles. The 1951 Evansville College graduate was inducted into the university's athletic Hall of Fame in 1996. He was named "Friend of the Year" for 1994 by the organization Friends of Bosse Field.

Braves slugger Joe Unfried. *Courtesy of Lois Unfried.*

Unfried put in a solid year, hitting 11 home runs (.264 BA), but the E-Braves drew an abysmal 47,144 at the gate. The off-season ushered in serious concerns about the stability of the league and specifically about the future of its longtime member city Evansville.

The Beginning of a Brave End

The Three-I League meetings convened at Chicago's Lake Shore Club in November. Seven of eight franchise owners said they would field teams in 1956, with only Terre Haute undecided. Evansville got a shock when Milwaukee clarified that its "yes" meant it would put a team in the Three-I "somewhere but not necessarily Evansville." Milwaukee just absorbed Evansville's $60,000 operating loss.

Evansville mayor H.O. Roberts convened a special committee to explore options to keep a professional team. A rent reduction and selling advertising space at the ballpark were top "do-able" proposals. Lynn Stone proposed selling beer. The ballpark was still governed by the school board, and it was lightening quick in saying no to beer. Mayor-elect Vance Hartke, a part of the special committee, said the city couldn't help with the rent. The board approved a one-year agreement allowing advertising in the park. The board cancelled the $4,865 annual rental contract and replaced it with a charge of $0.05 per paid admission, with a $1,600 annual minimum.

Joe Cairnes, executive vice-president of the Milwaukee Braves, turned down the rent offer. The offer was a three-year lease. With one year left on the current contract, Cairnes opted to play it out. Uneasiness about long-term viability of professional baseball in Evansville was still pervasive. The issue of beer at the ballpark kept raising its ugly head. The parent club promoted Lynn Stone to general manager of its Wichita AAA team in the American Association. His replacement, Austin Brown, came in after a year as business manager at Class-C Boise (Idaho) in the Pioneer League.

Prospects for 1956 were bright coming out of spring training in Waycross, Georgia. Joe Unfried was back, as was a more seasoned crooner and ballplayer, Lee Maye.

The season started with twenty-eight minor leagues. Nine teams either changed locations or disbanded during the season. One of those that disbanded was lifelong rival Terre Haute on July 3. Terre Haute president and owner Paul Frisz called it quits with the club 40-26 and in second place. Scheduling seven remaining teams was tricky. The clubs took turns being idle. Evansville was first. "I don't think I've been rained out as a player, manager or coach [on the Fourth of July] for the past 46 years," Coleman told the *Courier*.

The Braves played magnificently. Lee Maye's return was a smashing success. He now had six recordings, and one of them, "Truly," was a top seller. Flair Records paid him three cents for every record sold. From 1956 until his retirement from baseball in 1972, Lee's number-one vocation was baseball. His philosophy on the matter was simple. "I figure I have more time to make the grade as a singer," he said. "My voice may be better at 40 than it is at 20, but I don't see anybody up there in baseball shining at 40." He hit .330 and led the Three-I in runs scored, hits and RBIs. He also unloaded 24 homers to tie Preacher Williams's modern record. Lee Maye ended a thirteen-year major-league career with 1,109 hits and a .274 lifetime batting average.

A month into the season, Austin Brown acquired former Evansville Braves MVP Horace Garner from Augusta (Georgia) of the Class-A Sally League. Garner went on to win the Three-I League batting crown with a .354 average.

ANOTHER SPAHN?

A pair of right-handers helped the E-Braves roll through the Three-I season. The first drew comparisons to former Evansville Bee Warren Spahn. Twenty-year-old Don Nottebart's 18 wins earned him the league's Most Valuable Player award. He posted two more 18-win seasons at Atlanta (AA) and Louisville (AAA) before getting called up full time in 1961. After a couple of ordinary years with the big Braves, former Evansville and Milwaukee Braves teammate Don McMahon tipped off Houston Colt 45s management that Nottebart would be a steal. Houston general manager Paul Richards acted on the tip and acquired Nottebart after the 1962 season. Nottebart won four of five decisions before he took the mound in Colt Stadium on May 17, 1963, and no-hit the Philadelphia Phillies. Nottebart's gem was the first in franchise history. Former Evansville Brave Al Spangler tracked down a fly ball in left field for the final out.

The other right-hander came from hockey country. Claude Raymond was from Quebec. He grew up playing his country's national sport, but his hometown of Saint-Jean was close enough to the U.S. border that baseball was a huge part of the sports scene. His hometown had a team in the Canadian Provincial League. The bespectacled Raymond won nine games from the bullpen with a 2.57 ERA. "Frenchie" Raymond pitched twelve major-league seasons. In 449 games, he won 46 and lost only 33. His last playing year was 1971. Claude stayed in baseball, first as a radio analyst for the Montreal Expos and then as a television color commentator beginning

Pitchers Clair Hickman, Don Nottebart, Bob Botz and Dale Hendrickson. *Courtesy Willard Library Archives.*

in 1985 for the club. He ended his baseball career coaching with the Expos from 2002 to 2004.

Hitting and pitching fueled the Braves to run away with both halves of the Three-I season. No playoffs were needed. Players and coaches split up a total of $3,500—$2,000 for the regular season and $1,500 for winning both halves. At forty-six games over .500, Coleman's crew obliterated the Three-I and made a modest comeback at the box office, attracting 60,910 for sixty home games but below the 100,000 needed to break even.

SAVE THE MINORS

A committee of American and National League representatives recommended $500,000 be made available to help minor-league teams. Commissioner Ford Frick appointed a "Save the Minors" committee of six to administer the funds. The fact was that $500,000 spread across all the "needy" franchises didn't amount to much. Real change needed to come in other ways.

Milwaukee Braves representative Joe Cairnes met with the school board and asked for and got a one-year contract, ensuring that Evansville would play in 1957. At the same time, he announced that the franchise lost $45,000 for the year. The contract called for a flat rate of $1,000 plus $0.05 for every admission over 50,000. Cairnes stated, "we don't know if we will stay in Evansville after the 1957 season."

NAPBL president George Trautman maintained that 80 percent of minor-league clubs reported losses in 1956. The ailing minors shrank from fifty-nine leagues in 1949 to twenty-eight in 1956. The number of cities with teams fell from 448 to 213 during the period. Attendance went from 42 million to 17 million. The year 1959 began with twenty-seven leagues spread over 194 cities.

Once again, Coleman was working with a young and inexperienced team that didn't have the star power of the 1956 club, but he had a catcher who would make the Hall of Fame by poking fun at his own mediocre playing skills.

THE '57 CATCHERS: JUST A BIT OUTSIDE

Behind the plate for the season-opener was a twenty-two-year-old in his second year of pro ball. He went 1-5 in his debut with the team, giving him the same batting average after one game that he would later end a six-year major-league career with: .200. This was Bob Uecker, ladies and gentlemen.

It took little time for Uecker to exhibit his ambiguous skills. The opening paragraph of a May 2 special-report story to the *Courier* read, "Bob Uecker was both the hero and the goat" in a game at Davenport. As hero, he blasted a two-run homer in the top of the ninth to tie the score. In the bottom of the inning, he turned goat when a Davenport batter tried for a squeeze-play bunt and missed the ball, "as did Uecker," said the story, allowing a runner to score. Uecker lasted seventeen games and was sent to Eau Claire on May 27. He hit .238 with 3 home runs for the Braves.

Most of the catching duty fell to Jewish backstop Sid Goldfader. He was a three-sport athlete at Brandeis University in the early 1950s. Goldfader and twenty-year-old John Grace were the only two catchers entering a home game against Cedar Rapids on August 1. Going after a pitch in the dirt, Goldfader hurt his thumb and left the game. Backup Grace came in and took a foul tip straight into his Adam's apple. He took a seat. Coleman asked

The Braves '57 infield. From left: George Holder (*3B*), Gayle Moore (*SS*), Bob Jacobs (*2B*) and captain Billy Smith (*1B*). *Courtesy Willard Library Archives.*

for volunteers and saw a lone hand waving. It was that of shortstop Johnny Stratton, who finished the game behind the plate.

Coleman needed a real catcher while the other two recovered from their injuries. A thirty-two-year-old salesman for the Gulf Refining Company was seen catching for the Sunbeam team in the semipro I-K League in May. Coleman telephoned to inquire about his availability. The salesman said he just happened to have two weeks of vacation coming up and agreed to "vacation" as the Braves catcher. Ray Fletcher, who had played for Evansville in all or parts of four seasons in the late 1940s and early '50s, joined the club. He hadn't caught professionally for two years and had no intention of leaving his job. During the two-week sabbatical, Fletcher appeared in all fourteen games. He hit an admirable .211 and picked up some extra money. When vacation ended, the full-time catchers were ready. Fletcher went back to his day job. As he turned in his playing duds, miracles and tribulations were unfolding for the Braves and Evansville.

THE GRANDSTANDS

The Braves trailed Peoria by eight and a half games. There were doubts, however, that Peoria could hold on financially. Peoria general manager and field manager Vern Hoscheit said his team would disband unless home attendance increased enough to meet payroll before leaving on their next road trip. John Livingston, the club's president, indicated that the Yankees "helped out" before but couldn't be counted on again.

If the Chiefs folded, the E-Braves would win the league by default due to their eleven-and-a-half-game lead over third-place Davenport. But on August 21, Livingston announced that Peoria would finish the season. The declaration came after a home game that brought 1,177 fans to Peoria's home park. Attendees took up a collection of $500 for the team's benefit. That was enough to fund an upcoming trip to Burlington. With the show of faith, the parent Yankees guaranteed team salaries for the balance of the season.

Underneath the crumbling Bosse Field grandstands in August 1957. *Courtesy Willard Library Archives.*

Evansville was six and a half games behind when a bombshell was dropped on Bosse Field. A ten-man committee, representing the Southwestern Chapter of Professional Engineers, issued a report on the structural integrity of Bosse Field. The group presented their findings to the Evansville School Board. Not one of the engineers would give the grandstands a clean bill of health. Learning that a localized collapse of the main grandstands could occur at any time sent local baseball men into despair. "We may as well hang the black crepe on the door," manager Coleman told *Courier* columnist Joe Aaron. Ironically, a grandstand collapse in 1914 had helped Bosse Field come into existence. Now, the specter of a collapse could spell the end of baseball in Evansville. The plan was to put up temporary bleachers to finish the season.

The next day, engineer James Brown from Employers Mutual of Wausau was sent by the Milwaukee Braves to do his own inspection. His conclusion was that Bosse Field was safe for any crowd. He asked the board to reverse its decision. "The [Milwaukee] Braves are insured for one million dollars with my company and I'm not worried in the least bit," said Brown. "And if I'm not worried, my company isn't worried." Despite pleadings from the insurer, the board remained steadfast in its decision to close the grandstands. School board president James Morelock said the board would repair the stands by spring.

THE COMEBACK

The E-Braves lost to Burlington while Milwaukee's Mullen sat in the press box and stared at the shiny green chairbacks, all empty. The next night, "Big Smoke" Garner returned to the lineup after an ankle injury and banged two doubles and a single to power the E-Braves to a victory over Burlington. The club headed out on the road for six games at six and a half games back. After a twin-bill sweep at Cedar Rapids, Coleman's crew was four down. The Braves headed to Keokuk and picked up a half game on the staggering league leaders.

The Braves headed home for their final six home games—three each with Cedar Rapids and Peoria. Railroad ties were positioned to shore up seats on either side of the main entrance. The grandstands were opened for 1,695 in addition to the 450 box seats already in use.

The Braves won the first game on August 30. Peoria's lead was two and one-half games. Ron Piche's two-hit shutout completed a sweep over Cedar

Signing autographs in 1957. *Courtesy Willard Library Archives.*

Bob Coleman's last team celebrates in the locker room after winning the 1957 Three-I pennant. *Courtesy Willard Library Archives.*

Rapids. The Braves were one game back. Peoria's game with Keokuk was rained out. With only one open date before the final three games of the season, President Totten said that the game would not be rescheduled. Totten ordered Peoria and Davenport to play a game postponed on August 28, at either Peoria or Davenport, providing it had a bearing on the league championship. Totten said the Peoria-Davenport game took precedent because it happened first. Peoria came to Evansville for the final three home games of the year with a one-game lead.

Dale Hendrickson pitched a two-hitter to win on the twenty-ninth. The teams were in a virtual tie, with Evansville statistically two percentage points behind. The bolstered grandstands, box seats and bleachers held an encouraging crowd of 1,581. Cuban pitcher Tony Diaz followed with a nail-biting 5–4 victory. The crowd of 2,618 watched the Braves climb into first place by one game. There were 3,111 at the last home game, a loss. The teams remained in a virtual tie. Season attendance ended at 54,236. A *Courier* story contained telling statistics about baseball in Eau Claire, Wisconsin. Despite a 10 percent decline in attendance, concessions increased 30 percent over the prior year, due to the addition of beer to the menu.

The E-Braves visited Peoria for the final three games. Peoria traveled to Davenport for the Totten-ordered makeup game and came away winners, 7–2. Their lead was a half game. The stage was set for the Chief-Brave showdown. Noel Mickelsen took the hill for Evansville and gutted out a 6–4 win, his seventeenth of the season. The Braves were up by a half game. With a win in the next game, Evansville would take home the crown. If Peoria won, Sunday's winner would take the crown. Evansville was buzzing. Local radio station WGBF dispatched play-by-play announcer Marv Bates to call the final two games in Peoria. It was the first road broadcast since 1952.

On Saturday, September 7, Coleman's men blasted four home runs. Hendrickson and Diaz pitched brilliantly. The Braves blasted the Chiefs, 11–4. It was over. Evansville earned the $2,000 winner's check. Coleman won back-to-back Three-I championships for the first time in his career. Horace Garner slugged his way to a second consecutive batting crown, the first two-timer in league history. The thirty-one-year-old questioned whether he would continue playing. Despite a career batting average of .321 in ten minor-league seasons, Garner never made it to the majors.

Pitching carried the Braves. The team had only three future major-leaguers on the roster during the season. Of the three, only Ron Piche

From left: outfielders Bill Moss, Joe Trenary, Em Lindbeck and Horace Garner. *Courtesy Willard Library Archives.*

finished the year. The hurlers sported a team ERA of 2.86. Noel Mickelsen (17-5, 2.54), Hank Hemmerley (15-8, 2.36), Antonio "Tony" Diaz (13-6, 2.77) and Piche (11-8, 2.57) made up one of Coleman's best starting staffs ever.

Despite the heroics, the club reported a $42,000 operating loss. The school board offered a lease of $1 per year for a professional baseball team to use the field in 1958 as repair planning began.

THE END

On October 15, Milwaukee brass hosted a noontime lunch in the upstairs dining salon of Smitty's Steak House to break somber news. They told a small group of newspapermen, radio and television reporters, local businessmen and a religious leader that the Evansville Braves were no more. "I may get into mischief next summer without any baseball to see," lamented the Reverend J.F. Rake. "Our Baseball Marriage Ends" was the heading of Dan Scism's column.

"It's a real tough blow on me," Coleman told Scism, "I like Evansville and I know they like me." The veteran manager had made his home in the river town since 1938, when he helped bring professional baseball back to Evansville. "No place has ever been so nice to me."

Days after the announcement, Mayor Hartke and Fans Club president Paul Bonham were in Memphis at the invitation of Class-AA Southern Association president Charles Hurth to present Evansville's application for a berth in the league. The association's New Orleans franchise was in doubt after it lost use of City Park Stadium at the end of the season. Hartke and Bonham told Hurth that Bosse Field repairs could be completed in time for Evansville to fill New Orleans' spot. In November, New Orleans worked out a deal to play in City Park Stadium and return to the SA.

Bonham presented an application to join the SA at the minor-league meetings in December. Hartke said that Bosse Field would "possibly" be ready by April 1. Bonham wasn't on the same page. He wouldn't guarantee readiness before July 1. Bonham made use of the networking opportunity to speak with Lee McPhail, Yankees director of player personnel. McPhail told Bonham to write him when Bosse Field was renovated. Walter Shannon of the St. Louis Cardinals told Bonham the same thing.

Architect Ralph Legeman presented plans for the restoration. They called for pre-cast concrete supports for five thousand permanent seats; work on roof supports; press box improvements; rewiring; and rebuilding of the restrooms, dressing rooms and showers. Legeman placed repair estimates at $345,000. The board voted to accept a petition for a bond issue of $375,000 and announced that bids would be taken. Renovation bids came in approximately $33,000 more than the bond issue. The field was the home for two high school football teams and many other civic and sporting events, so they had to proceed.

6

THE FIELD, THE SEARCH, THE ESOX AND THE GLOBAL FLOP

1958–69

Is It Worthwhile?

The minor leagues were deteriorating while Evansville fans wondered whether seeking a professional team was worthwhile. Dan Scism opined that the city "may be blowing a bundle" refurbishing Bosse Field if the sole reason was the return of organized baseball. The outlook got murkier in late January when Mayor Vance Hartke announced he was running for U.S. Senate in Indiana. His thoughts turned to politics over baseball.

Restoration progressed at a snail's pace, resulting in complaints about bid-winning Three-A Builders. A traditional Thanksgiving Day football game between North and Central High Schools was moved from Bosse Field to Enlow Field due to continuing construction. The missed season was followed by several years of near misses attempting to acquire a team.

Evansville had its sights on the Southern Association, but direction changed in August when Dan Scism wrote that "a baseball man" told him Evansville had a chance of getting a franchise in the AAA American Association if certain minor-league realignment developed. Scism wrote that three things had to happen for Evansville to be considered. First, the field needed to be ready. Second, parking needed to be expanded. The third was a recurring theme: concessions stands had to sell beer.

Three-I League president Hal Totten wanted to expand to eight teams and invited Evansville to league meetings in late November, but the appetite

Repairs of the Bosse Field grandstand began in 1958. *Courtesy Willard Library Archives.*

for Class-B baseball was gone. No one attended. Bob Coleman returned from his 1958 journeys as a Milwaukee special-assignment operative in September and weighed in on the chance for a AAA team. He said there was "no chance" until the sale of beer was permitted.

THE OLD MARSE EXITS

After spring training broke, Evansville selected mayoral candidates. William Davidson led a slate of Democrats in the May primaries that included sitting Vanderburgh County sheriff Frank McDonald and a forty-year-old war hero named Walter Dilbeck. The flamboyant Dilbeck ran for the office in the 1955 primary and received 539 votes. This time, Dilbeck campaigned on a mule and handed out free barbecue in local saloons and garnered 568 votes. The forty-six-year-old McDonald won the primary and the mayoral contest in November.

Bob Coleman, dubbed the "Old Marse," started his golden anniversary year in baseball with the enthusiasm of a rookie. He was sixty-eight years old and showing no signs of stopping a career that started as a catcher in 1910. But Coleman lost his appetite for food while on the road in May and lost nearly thirty pounds in three weeks. He returned to Evansville for a physical and underwent abdominal surgery at St. Mary's Hospital on June 5. After a week in the hospital, he returned home feeling "alright." Within weeks, he requested to be sent back to St. Mary's, where he was listed in serious condition.

Milwaukee owner Lou Perini sent his personal plane to Evansville's Dress Memorial Airport on July 14 to transport Coleman to Boston for tests. Coleman was accompanied by Austin Brown, former business manager of the E-Braves. The results were grim. Coleman had pancreatic cancer too advanced to treat. He died the next day at 6:45 a.m. in Boston's Peter Bent Brigham Hospital near Harvard University.

Funeral services were conducted in Evansville before his burial in St. Joseph's Cemetery on July 21. Accolades and condolences poured in from a who's who of professional baseball. Commissioner Ford Frick called Coleman a baseball man whose "popularity wasn't often rivaled." Former commissioner and current Kentucky governor A.B. "Happy" Chandler recalled his "unfailing kindness to my father." Chandler's father rarely missed Evansville Braves games. The Chandlers lived on Outer Newburgh Road, and the governor played baseball in Evansville as a boy. Evansville baseball alumni, such as Johnny Logan and Warren Spahn, spoke warmly of Coleman. Casey Stengel said that "he was a man who could do almost everything in baseball." The nationwide reaction was overwhelming.

Coleman was prolific as a manager. At his death, he had more victories than any minor-league manager in history with 2,496. Counting wins as a major-league manager, playoff wins and a one-year winter instructional league stint brought the total to nearly 2,700. His final two Three-I League championships brought his Evansville total to four. Coleman also won a Three-I League championship as manager of Terre Haute in 1922.

The Southern Association Beckons

George Trautman was looking for ideas to save the minor-league system in 1959 when a man named William Shea came on the scene. Shea was appointed by New York mayor Robert Wagner to bring baseball back to New York after Dodger and Giant defections. The major leagues had not expanded since 1900, and Commissioner Frick was encouraging teams to curtail moves. Without a pathway to a team, Shea came up with the idea of a new major league called the Continental League and recruited Branch Rickey to help. Trautman was livid. The Continental League would dip into the minors for talent and crush minor-league towns.

The Southern Association showed local interest again in September 1959. Birmingham Barons general manager Eddie Glennon said Evansville was a "likely" SA franchise in 1960. Fred Russell, sports editor of the *Nashville Banner*, concurred with Glennon. Skeptics jumped in. "Is Evansville a prospect or will a bottle of beer keep Class-AA baseball out of Evansville?" asked *Courier and Press* columnist Hap Glaudi. "All you have to do is ice up a few" to secure a team. The city was again without organized baseball in 1960.

Hal Totten took over the Southern Association presidency in 1960. Russwood Park, home of the SA's Memphis Chicks, burned to the ground before the 1960 season. Evansville was in the mix, but a "test run" of five Chicks games in Columbus (Georgia) was successful enough to make that city the new target. In July, major-league owners offered expansion franchises to New York and Houston. In a matter of weeks, Shea and Rickey announced that they were abandoning Continental League plans. The crisis was averted for Trautman and the minor leagues. Trautman announced that minor-league attendance had dipped by more than 1.1 million.

Baseball possibilities revived in April 1961 when Wilbur Clippinger, president of the Evansville Board of Education, was contacted by the Southern Association about using Bosse Field. An attorney, Isadore Newman, told Clippinger that he had a client interested in the SA's failing Macon (Georgia) club and wanted to know if the field could be obtained. At midseason, another franchise, Mobile, was up for grabs. Evansville "interests" contacted Southern Association officials asking for a franchise. Nothing happened.

Los Angeles Dodgers vice-president Buzzi Bavasi, a DePauw University graduate, announced that its Atlanta Southern Association franchise would be in the AAA International League next season or their Class-AA club would leave there. Bavasi had issues with the Southern Association's restrictions against black players. Totten encouraged Bavasi to move the Atlanta franchise to Evansville. Attorney Isadore Newman had not heard anything on the subject he had brought to the board of education earlier that summer. A few weeks later, the *Courier* learned the name of at least one of Newman's baseball clients. It was Walter Dilbeck.

Private Dilbeck's Other Wars

Dilbeck was born in Fort Riley, Kansas, where his father was a major in the army. He was the oldest of nine children. Shortly after his birth, the family moved to Fort Branch, where he played on the high school basketball and baseball teams and even got a tryout with the St. Louis Cardinal organization in 1935. He was also an amateur boxer. As a teenager, he worked at Swift & Company, the meatpacking company in Evansville, and worked his way from "cellar boy" to a spot in the company's business administration school. He married his wife, Dorothy, when he was twenty. In 1943, he was drafted in the army and sent to fight with the Sixty-Third Infantry Division in Europe.

During the storming of the Siegfried Line, Dilbeck displayed one of the single most remarkable examples of courage and valor. As an army private in 1945, near Buchof, Germany, Dilbeck single-handedly held off more than two hundred German SS soldiers while killing sixty. It made him one of the nation's most decorated World War II soldiers and a genuine war hero. His World War II heroism earned two Distinguished Service Crosses with Valor, four Bronze Stars and four Purple Hearts. After the war, Dilbeck returned to Chicago and his job at Swift and branched out into real estate, buying and selling tracts of land. He made a fortune.

The Dodgers

Totten and Birmingham GM Glennon came to town in early November to discuss putting a AA team in Evansville. A Dilbeck-arranged Holiday Inn meeting went well enough. Totten said he wanted $50,000 in the bank before selling a ticket. Isadore Newman inquired about adding outfield advertising and beer concession at a school board meeting. As for beer, he said, "I don't think we'll get very far" but that every other team in the league sold beer. Totten and Glennon said they would inform the Dodgers of Evansville's interest.

Mayor McDonald conferred with the Dodgers and made a ticket-sale pledge of $60,000. Dilbeck's group dropped out because the school board refused to grant them a contract. McDonald's group informed the mayor they couldn't finance a team, leaving him no option but to find a major-league team to run the operation. McDonald met with Buzzi Bavasi and

Dodger farm director Frisco Thompson, as well as other Los Angeles club officials. At the end of the meeting, Evansville had a team.

"The Evansville Mayor sold us," said a Dodgers official. "He gave us more incentive to let his city have our [Atlanta] franchise than any other city." The Dodgers would provide the field manager, the business manager and the operating personnel. One question remained. Would the Southern Association operate in 1962? The league was down to five teams and needed six. One positive was that Southern Association officials recently voted to allow Negroes to play in the league.

The Associated Press reported a "strong possibility" that the Southern Association and the Sally (South Atlantic) League would merge. The clock was ticking for the Southern Association and Evansville's dream association with the Dodgers. Days later, things fell apart. The two Southern Association Tennessee cities—Nashville and Chattanooga—bolted to the Sally League. The Class-AA Southern Association had to close shop.

MORE LEAGUE INTRIGUE

Baseball banter started again in June 1962. The AAA American Association was down to six teams after losing several cities to the major leagues (Minneapolis, for instance). Evansville was mentioned as a likely member to shore up the league. Mayor McDonald had his plane ticket for the minor-league meetings in Rochester, New York. McDonald said he thought he could get Evansville into the South Atlantic League (Sally), and there was a possibility of making the American Association with the support of the Washington Senators. After a few phone calls with potential suitors, he decided to cancel the trip to Rochester. He missed quite a show.

On day one, minor-league representatives voted to collapse the three AAA leagues into two. The second day, the American Association was the odd league out. Only the Pacific Coast and International Leagues survived. A joint committee of major- and minor-league representatives voted to reorganize the minor-league classification system. The system was torn apart and rebuilt. Teams once classified as B, C and D were abolished and all renamed Class-A. The reorganized minors were lumped into AAA, AA, A and Class-A Rookie. Twenty teams were guaranteed at both the AAA and AA levels. The other sixty were guaranteed for Class-A and Class-A Rookie. After deciding the two AAA leagues, the Eastern, Sally and Texas made up Class-AA.

The American Association wasn't dead yet. The far-flung nature of the International League was sapping travel budgets. The Associated Press wrote of an August story from Chicago, where a major-minor executive council approved a plan to reactivate the American Association with six clubs. The plan would return the International and Pacific Coast Leagues to eight teams each and reform the American Association without eliminating any current clubs. Evansville was at the forefront of candidate cities, but the idea withered away.

McDonald headed to the baseball winter meetings in San Diego knowing of a potential open franchise. Little Rock dropped out of the International League. The St. Louis Cardinals were one of three major-league teams interested in Evansville. No sooner had McDonald arrived than he learned the International League decided to drop to eight teams. Little Rock and Indianapolis departed for the Pacific Coast League, which grew to twelve teams.

McDonald said the Cardinals still "definitely" wanted to place a franchise in Evansville. They told him they preferred Evansville over Portland. The major-league meetings were the following week in Los Angeles, where the Cardinals hoped to push for realignment of the two Class-AAA leagues back to ten teams each, with Evansville and Indianapolis joining the International League. Evansville lost again. Commissioner Frick said that teams that fielded AAA teams the previous season should have the first chance to join. That opened the door for Jacksonville, Florida, a city jilted when Cleveland grabbed Portland as its top farm city. St. Louis took Jacksonville.

While the Milwaukee Braves delayed a move to Atlanta, Evansville was discussed as the replacement for Atlanta in the International League. IL president Tommy Richardson stated that his league would take up the Atlanta replacement situation midway through 1965. "We'd like to do business with your Mayor McDonald," said Richardson.

Basketball Is King

In the early spring of 1965, the buzz in the Pocket City was basketball. The Evansville College basketball team, led by All-American Jerry Sloan, finished an undefeated season and took home its fourth NCAA College Division National Championship (now called Division II) under future Hall of Fame Coach Arad McCutchan. The school and town reached the pinnacle of national fame, garnering feature stories in *Sports Illustrated* throughout the season after defeating the likes of Notre Dame, UCLA and Iowa. The sports world knew Evansville.

Richmond, Virginia, grabbed Atlanta's spot in the International League. Options were drying up, so Walter Dilbeck wanted to fill the void with a Stan Musial League team in Evansville. The Musial League was for players over eighteen, with no upward age limit. There were already Musial Leagues in Muncie, Fort Wayne and Indianapolis. Dilbeck put together an entry by July 15 in order to be eligible for the national tournament in Battle Creek, Michigan. The Musial Leagues attracted former college, semipro and minor-league players of all ages.

Dilbeck's team was named the Riflemen. He knew he needed star power, and he got it. Two Riflemen were members of the Evansville College basketball team, Rick Kingston and Jerry Mattingly. Mattingly led the league in hitting for the unbeaten Riflemen. Dilbeck announced plans to enlarge the league beyond Evansville to sixteen teams in 1966. He wanted to purchase eighteen acres of land on the northwest side of Evansville to construct four lighted diamonds. As his team readied for the August Musial League state tournament in Fort Wayne, another possibility of professional baseball's return popped up.

PAY DIRT

"The man who owns the Birmingham park is going to sell it," Southern League president Sam Smith said. Smith said that Chattanooga was another Southern League city in trouble and suggested that one franchise could move to Evansville. Smith stated flatly that the Southern League would operate with eight teams in 1966. He had feelers out to Nashville, Evansville, Memphis and Mobile.

Another Southern League city, Lynchburg (Virginia), announced that it was leaving for the Class-A Carolina League. Lynchburg was the Chicago White Sox Class-AA representative. The franchise struggled with travel in the expansive SL and opted for the more compact Carolina League. The big club wanted to keep Lynchburg as its Class-A team. Macon filled Chattanooga's spot. It was almost certain that Mobile would take Birmingham's spot.

Two weeks later, the path to professional baseball brightened. Mayor McDonald said, "They [the White Sox] came to see me. I didn't seek

Mayor Frank McDonald Sr.
Courtesy Willard Library Archives.

them out." The mayor said that White Sox representatives were coming to discuss the matter. The oft-burned city leader kept his expectations in check. In early December, the *Courier* broke the news with the headline "Organized Baseball Will Return Here Next Spring." Evansville was now one hop away from the big leagues. That hop was through Indianapolis, the White Sox AAA franchise in the Pacific Coast League.

Walter Dilbeck had mixed emotions. He wanted to support the city's new team but had put together a 152-game Musial League schedule that included 96 games split between Lamasco and Bosse Fields for the coming year. Equipment and uniforms had been ordered for 240 players in the new Musial setup. He wasn't left completely holding the bag, however, as he pointed out that "the Government" was paying 75 percent of the cost.

Franchise owners Tom Fleming and William Ackerman hailed from South Carolina. Fleming, a Northwestern University English literature graduate, had recorded twelve straight years in the minor leagues without losing money in any one of them. Fleming took an active role as general manager. Ackerman, an attorney, was a silent partner and served as president. They co-owned the Lynchburg franchise before the move. Fleming had never seen Bosse Field before he visited Evansville. After a tour of the facility, he said, "You can't find anything better, anywhere."

PREPARATIONS

The Evansville White Sox were dubbed the Esox. Tom Fleming chose a business manager with a name familiar to those who had followed the E-Braves during the forties and fifties. Ray Fletcher, who had vacationed as a catcher for the Evansville Braves in 1957, was named business manager. A former shortstop for the Quincy Gems in the 1950s was named field manager. Thirty-eight-year-old George Noga guided Lynchburg to the Southern League championship in 1964. Fletcher, now forty-one, had settled in Evansville over a decade earlier. His job was to sell tickets. He was in a home-building business partnership when Fleming tabbed him for the job.

The Southern League was a bus-riding circuit. Evansville's nearest rival was Knoxville, 353 highway miles away. Mobile was the farthest from Evansville at 601 miles. That equated to a fourteen-hour bus ride with stops included. There were no easy trips.

The White Sox opened offices in Bosse Field. Fletcher reported that more than half of the 435 box seats had been sold by early February. At month's end, all box seats were gobbled up. The team had nearly $40,000 in the bank before a single player was known to the public. The club had a player development agreement with the Chicago White Sox that provided players, a portion of salaries, spring training expenses and three of the four sets of uniforms.

The obligatory question of beer sales was put to the new general manager. Fleming, a fifty-seven-year-old with twenty years of minor-league experience, handled the question with perfect aplomb. "We didn't have beer in Lynchburg, but I must say that more beer and whiskey were consumed in the park than in some of the other league parks where it [beer] was sold." Fleming said he would make no attempt to discuss beer again while the field was controlled by the school board.

A twenty-six-player roster included several holdovers from the Class-AA Lynchburg team of 1965. In early April, Dick Littleton, a scrappy second baseman, was picked up from Indianapolis. Littleton signed for a $40,000 bonus by the Cleveland Indians in 1962. Another former bonus baby pickup was Danny Murphy. He signed with the Cubs for $100,000 in 1960 as an outfielder and was being converted to a pitcher by the White Sox.

Fleming arranged an April 9 exhibition game between the Cincinnati Reds and the Chicago White Sox. The Saturday afternoon contest drew 5,719 fans, overflowing the 5,000 permanent seats. The Bosse Field throng watched the White Sox down the Reds, 5–1. Pete Rose went hitless in four trips to the plate for the Reds.

PLAYERS AND VIETNAM

Vietnam had an impact on player availability after 1964, when the war and draft escalated. Most players eligible for the draft entered reserve programs, predominately with the U.S. Army Reserves. Basic training and required

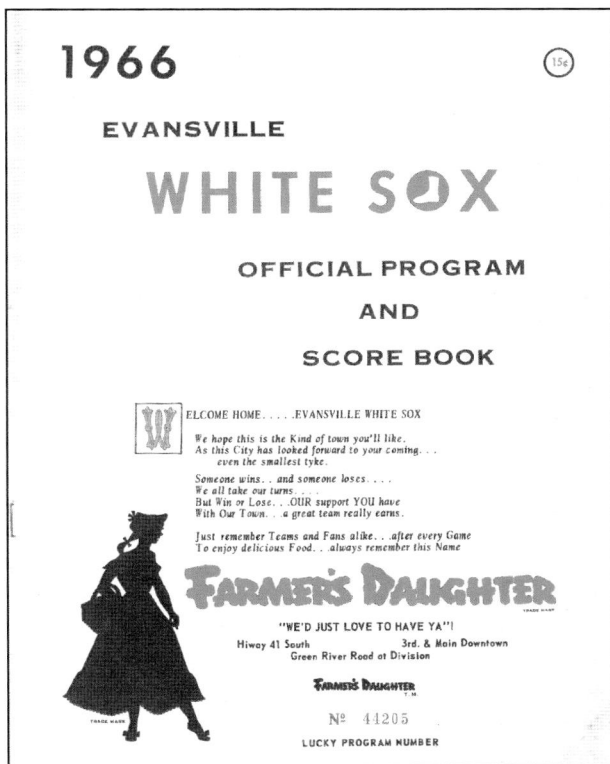

The Evansville White Sox first season program. *Author's collection.*

meetings often took players away from the field. Arguably the new team's best pitcher [Roger Nelson] and player [Buddy Bradford] reported for three weeks of duty at the California National Guard Camp near Monterrey, California, at the end of July.

At the Class-AA level, players were considered prospects. Southern League president Sam Smith explained that Class-AA was sort of a make-it-or-break-it level of minor-league baseball. "The Southern League is a point of separation for baseball players," said Smith. "If a player clicks in this league, he's at the major league door with a good chance of entering. If they can't go in this league, they'd best find non-baseball employment."

An example was the contrast between two of the club's outfielders, Jesse Queen and Buddy Bradford. Queen was a veteran of the minor leagues who had started in the Tiger organization in 1956 and made it all the way to AAA. He was twenty-nine years old. He was peddled to the White Sox organization in 1964 and put together two mediocre seasons at AA Lynchburg. Bradford was a prospect.

Bradford signed with the White Sox for $8,000 in 1962 and climbed steadily through the organization, reaching AAA Indianapolis in 1965. He was only twenty-one years old. Bradford possessed a quick bat and ran like the wind, having once been clocked at a time of 9.7 or 9.9 seconds in the 100-yard dash, depending on which report you believed. He had a strong arm. "As strong as anyone in the White Sox organization," said Chicago manager Eddie Stanky in the spring. Buddy was on the way up.

A CHILLING DEBUT

Chilly weather and a daylong threat of rain kept many away as the Esox faced Knoxville on opening night. The April 21 game attracted a disappointing paid crowd of only 2,080 for an 8:00 p.m. start. Among the overcoat-wearing attendees was eighty-three-year-old Ned Crowder of Zanesville, Ohio, believed to be the oldest surviving member of an Evansville professional baseball team. He played shortstop for the River Rats from 1907 to 1909. The 1908 team was Central League champions under Punch Knoll. The Esox won, 7–1.

Injuries plagued Evansville the first two months of the season, and the team sputtered to a 20-34 record by mid-June. The most disabling injury came six games into the season and struck down promising shortstop Rich Morales. In a Bosse Field game against Asheville on April 27, the twenty-two-year-old Morales caught a short fly ball to center field and tripped over Bradford, who was trying to get out of the way. The result was a torn lateral ligament in his right knee, requiring surgery. Morales was out for the year. The club averaged 1,200 paid attendance through the first dozen games when start times moved from 8:00 p.m. to 7:30 p.m. to encourage more school-aged attendees.

A sluggish start ended with a doubleheader sweep of the Columbus Confederate Yankees on the Fourth of July in Georgia. Esox righty Cisco Carlos tossed a 3–0 shutout in the first seven-inning game. In the nightcap, lefty Steve Jones faced the minimum of twenty-one opposing batters, struck out 9 and recorded the first no-hit game by an Evansville pitcher since Dick Manville aced Davenport in 1947. The sweep was not out of the ordinary for this club. In 1966, it set the all-time Southern League record in one season with seven.

The 1966 Evansville White Sox. *Courtesy Willard Library Archives.*

ED HERRMANN

Nineteen-year-old Ed Herrmann was advanced to Evansville by the White Sox to shore up the catching. Ed was described in the March 1968 special of *Baseball Digest* as a player who "can't hit enough to make him a big leaguer." He proved that scouting report wrong.

Herrmann had a good and accurate arm. His baseball lineage included a tidbit for trivia aficionados. His grandfather Marty "Lefty" Herrmann pitched a single inning for the Brooklyn Robins [later named Dodgers] during the 1918 season. Born in Oldenburg, Indiana, Lefty was a plumber and semipro pitcher in Cincinnati during World War I. Brooklyn manager Wilbert Robinson's pitching staff had nine hurlers join the armed services by the end of the year. Robinson was desperate for pitching coming into a July 10 doubleheader in Cincinnati and saw Marty Herrmann pitching a semipro game. Robinson signed him in time to suit up for the first game at Redland Field [renamed Crosley in 1934]. At the top of the seventh inning,

Catcher Ed Herrmann in his Esox home whites. *Author's collection.*

Robinson motioned for the twenty-five-year-old plumber from the bullpen. Marty Herrmann pitched a hitless inning, walking 1 batter and holding the Reds scoreless. At the end of the second game of the doubleheader, Lefty Herrmann was released.

Grandson Ed built a reputation as an ironman who insisted on playing every day, no matter what. He was also referred to as "Fort Herrmann" for his ability to block the plate. His toughness led him to an eleven-year major-league career.

The Cisco Kid

Evansville had clawed its way back to one game below .500 and in third place behind Mobile and Asheville before the Southern League All-Star Game in Mobile. Those two teams had distanced themselves from the rest of the pack. Esox manager George Noga skippered the All-Stars against the first-place Mobile A's. Mobile was so stacked with talent that it wasn't much of a game. Sal Bando blasted a home run for Mobile in the 6–1 rout. Rick Monday led off for the home team. Tony LaRussa was at second base. Future Pittsburgh Pirates Bob Robertson, Al Oliver and Dock Ellis highlighted the All-Star roster. Noga had one of his own on the team, pitcher Cisco Carlos, who pitched a scoreless eighth inning.

Carlos was the top hurler in the Evansville White Sox pitching stable. The Cisco Kid, as he was called, was a tall, twenty-five-year-old righty in his sixth professional season. This was the "make or break" stage of his baseball career. His 15-8 won-loss record and sparkling ERA of 2.58 tilted the scales in the "make" direction.

Before the 1968 season began, Cisco appeared on the covers of *Sports Illustrated* and *Baseball Digest*. He shared both covers with "rookie sensation" Johnny Bench. He appeared on a Topps rookie baseball card. By the end of 1970, he had pitched his last big-league game, then with Washington. Carlos finished with a career record of 11-18.

Corky Comes Home

Noga and Carlos greeted a local celebrity when they returned after the break. Corky Withrow was back. The colorful Central City (Kentucky) athlete, who starred in high school and then college basketball at Georgetown College in Kentucky, was an instant hit. After riding the bench most of the 1966 season for Syracuse in the International League, he left at his own request and asked that he be sent to Evansville, which was just seventy miles from his Kentucky home.

Corky was happy to be back in Evansville and especially liked playing for George Noga. Within the next couple of weeks, he announced that this season would be his last. "I've spent too many years playing behind guys I should have been playing ahead of, so I've had it," he told the *Courier and Press*. Except for six games with the St. Louis Cardinals in

1963, he labored eleven seasons in the minors and played in over 1,100 games. Withrow is the only player to appear in both Evansville Braves and White Sox uniforms. He had one at bat with the E-Braves after signing in 1957.

EVERYDAY ED

The Esox season ended with a day-night doubleheader. Because the two games were split into two paying events, each game was nine innings rather than the usual seven innings for twin bills. The Sox won the daytime affair and dropped the nightcap to Montgomery. A plucky right-handed reliever won the first and lost the second. The finale was the sixtieth appearance of the season for "Everyday Ed" Nottle.

It wasn't unusual for Nottle to work consecutive games. He relieved in three straight games earlier in the season and won them all. The uninterrupted pitching victories over Charlotte (July 8–10) were believed to be the Southern League record for most successive wins. Ed accomplished the feat again two years later. He appeared in seventy-five games for the 1968 Esox. From May 30 through June 1, he notched another three in a row against Asheville twice and Montgomery once.

Nottle's minor-league pitching career spanned 543 appearances from 1960 to 1976 with a record of 89 wins and 75 losses. Nottle managed 3,024 minor-league games before calling it quits in 2008. He spent many of his off-seasons and retirement singing in clubs but was never far away from a baseball field. He coached the Bosse High School baseball team for a short time in the early 1990s. Nottle remained an Evansville resident after his professional baseball days.

ANOTHER SEASON GUARANTEED

The Esox took third place with a record of 68-72. Success was measured in more than just wins and losses. Evansville led the Southern League in attendance by a large margin with a paid attendance of 69,697. Tom Fleming was named Class-AA Executive of the Year by the *Sporting News* in December.

Chico Fernandez topped Evansville with a .302 average. Chico was on the edge at age twenty-seven with already eight years in the minors. In 1968, he finally made a major-league roster. Fernandez spent the entire season with Baltimore as a utility infielder, appearing in 24 games. He retired from playing in 1969. Buddy Bradford led the club with 13 home runs. Jesse Queen was the ironman of the team. Playing both infield and outfield positions, Queen appeared in 135 of the 140 games and hit a solid .278. Pitchers Steve Jones, Roger Nelson and converted outfielder Danny Murphy threw well enough to keep their names on the big-league radar screen. Murphy also smacked 5 home runs.

The Southern League was in flux when the season ended. President Sam Smith was hoping to field eight teams in 1967 but was "positive" he would have six. With six, each team would play 28-game schedules against member teams instead of 20 each to get to a 140-game season. It meant four trips to each city rather than three. Smith said Evansville, Macon, Charlotte, Montgomery, Knoxville and Birmingham were in.

Dilbeck's Dream

Walter Dilbeck's Stan Musial League dream died, but he kept the Dilbeck Riflemen and shelled out nearly $25,000 on them in 1966. They breezed through their thirty-one-game schedule unblemished, bringing their two-season total to fifty-two consecutive regular-season victories. They dropped the first game of the double-elimination Indiana State Championship but coasted to the title after that. In early October, he announced his next baseball venture.

Dilbeck represented a group of Milwaukee attorneys that attempted to purchase the Kansas City A's from Charlie O. Finley in early 1966. Finley toyed with the idea before but passed. Dilbeck huffed that Finley's franchise wasn't worth half of what they offered and decided it was time for a third major league. When reminded of William Shea's Continental League drama, Dilbeck said the country wasn't ready then but was ready now.

Dilbeck had been floating the idea to representatives of large U.S. cities without teams for some time. He said Seattle, St. Paul, Dallas, Indianapolis, Miami, Denver, Memphis and Atlanta were interested, as were the Philippines and Puerto Rico. Eleven cities accepted invitations to discuss his concept on October 20–21 at Evansville's Hotel McCurdy.

He asked each city for $50,000 to get things started. A hopeful Dilbeck said the group would elect officers and use $500,000 to operate the league in 1968. He proposed a twelve-team league of two divisions, with each team having two affiliate clubs as his version of the minors. The representatives drafted a declaration of intent and agreed on a name: the Global League.

Retired *Courier* sports editor Dan Scism joined Dilbeck and Associates as vice-president of the personnel department in January 1967. Scism worked out of Dilbeck's downtown Ramada Inn offices. The confident millionaire announced that he would award eight franchises at a meeting in Phoenix. City representatives needed to bring $50,000 for a franchise. His most recent list included Phoenix, Chicago, Milwaukee, San Diego, Dallas, New York, Montreal and Puerto Rico and possibly Manila and Tokyo.

Seven cities paid deposits at the Phoenix meeting. The ever-changing list now included Jersey City, Phoenix, Indianapolis, Milwaukee, New York, Dallas and San Diego. Manila verbally committed but brought no money. Dilbeck kicked in the entry fee for Indianapolis. Dilbeck said five more franchises would be awarded by April 1 so that twelve teams would play in 1968. Max Schumacher, general manager of the Indianapolis Indians, predicted that Dilbeck's third major league would be a fiasco. Dilbeck shrugged off Schumacher's comment, telling the *Evansville Press* he had $150,000 on deposit locally and another $50,000 "in my pocket" from Phoenix. The math didn't equal seven teams.

After Phoenix, he was in Omaha for a tour of Rosenblatt Stadium. Dilbeck talked about doubling its capacity to 35,000 seats. During a meandering press conference, he said he talked with an interested Mickey Mantle about managing a Dallas entry. Pressed on the question of acquiring talent, Dilbeck said he'd buy major-league players. A day later, the Associated Press reported that the Toronto Maple Leafs turned down an offer to join the Global League. Leafs president Bob Hunter wondered how Dilbeck would find players. Meanwhile, Dan Scism said the Global League agreed on a ninety-day option on Milwaukee's County Stadium, but it was later rejected by a county commission.

A pamphlet began arriving in newspaper sports departments across the country titled "Play Ball." It was subtitled "The Official Publication of the Global League." Under the masthead showing Evansville as headquarters was the headline "Global League Moves Towards 1968 Opening."

At a Dallas meeting in February, Dilbeck claimed he had six cities with "tentative" agreements to lease stadiums. Now it was Jersey City, Omaha, the Carolinas (Charlotte), Louisville, Indianapolis and Dallas–Fort Worth. Dilbeck "anticipated" clubs from Japan, Manila, Mexico and possibly Puerto Rico. The stadium deals were sketchy. One was Turnpike Stadium near Dallas, where there was a dispute between the owner and the prospective Global League franchise owner as to whether an agreement letter was really an agreement. The Carolinas intended to use Charlotte Motor Speedway. Dilbeck said he was attempting to buy stock of the Indianapolis Indians to gain use of their stadium.

Only Jersey City and Omaha seemed legitimate. Roosevelt Stadium, home of the Brooklyn Dodgers for fifteen games during 1956 and 1957, seated 24,000 and was leased to the Global League, according to Jersey City mayor Jimmy Whelan. For the first time, Dilbeck's confidence wavered on the league start date. When the discussion turned to acquiring players, Dilbeck remained confident but nebulous. "If we have young men coming out of college that can learn to fly airplanes upside down in Vietnam and to play professional football, then they can play major league baseball too," said Dilbeck.

The Esox Opening Day game program contained a full-page ad with a picture of the mustachioed Walter J. Dilbeck extending best wishes to the Southern League from the Global League, but in late June, Dilbeck speculated that the league debut might be pushed to 1969. The list of cities submitting $50,000 guarantees was down to four: Jersey City, Dallas, Phoenix and Puerto Rico, with a "promise" from Charlotte and Indianapolis. He said Rosenblatt Stadium was guaranteed. By his count, there were seven "committed" teams, and negotiations with Portland and Seattle were underway.

THE BEST SOX

The Evansville White Sox were ten games over .500 and two and a half games behind the league-leading Montgomery Rebels when Global League talk slowed in 1967. Five Esox players made the Southern League All-Star Game against the Atlanta Braves on June 26 at Charlotte's Clark Griffith Park. Three Evansville pitchers—Mickey Abarbanel, Greg Bollo and Ray Cordeiro—made the roster, along with first sacker Gary Johnson and catcher Ed Herrmann. Noga was voted by the league to manage the All-Stars.

Esox 1967 pitchers, from left: Ray Cordeiro, Mickey Abarbanel, Danny Murphy, Greg Bollo and Scott Seger. *Author's collection.*

Bollo and Abarbanel were flamethrowers. The former was a right-hander, the latter a southpaw. Bollo was in his fourth year of professional baseball and had done two stints with the big-league Sox, appearing in 18 games over 1965 and 1966. Michael Gary "Mickey" Abarbanel was drafted fifty-seventh overall by the White Sox in the 1965 amateur draft. In his first full year in Class-A, he struck out 206 batters in 144 innings. A 15-strikeout outing for the 1967 Esox opened eyes in the organization. Both Abarbanel and Bollo were prospects. Bollo never made it back to the bigs, and Abarbanel never made it at all.

Sam Smith's stars shut out the Atlanta Braves, 5–0. Greg Bollo started the game with two perfect innings and was given the win. Rico Carty was picked off first by starting catcher Ed Herrmann as Hank Aaron was leaving home plate after striking out. Smith was able to announce the official attendance of 6,554 and said he hoped to make the game an annual attraction.

BELTIN' MELTON

Californian Bill Melton never played organized amateur baseball. In 1964, he played baseball on weekends on a field by the Rose Bowl where local minor-league players often practiced. White Sox scout Hollis Thurston saw him hit 2 home runs in one game and asked him if he'd consider professional baseball. Having just graduated from high school, and needing a summer job, the eighteen-year-old signed and headed to Sarasota, Florida, to play for the White Sox Rookie League team.

The White Sox sent him to Evansville to become a third baseman. The experiment was brutal. The twenty-year-old committed 29 errors and batted a tepid .251 with only 9 long balls. White Sox scouts following him saw what box scores didn't reflect. He hit many long outs to the wall of Bosse Field's cavernous four-hundred-foot left center field power alley. The smashes would have been home runs in any other park. The Chicago White Sox made him their full-time third baseman in 1969.

The slugger's fan base expanded in 1971. He made the American League All-Star Game and engaged in a battle for the league home run title with Detroit's Norm Cash and former Southern League rival Reggie Jackson and then with Oakland. The three were tied at 32 entering the final day of the season. In his second at-bat, Melton turned on a fastball. The ball sailed into the left-field stands. For the first time ever, the White Sox had the leading home run hitter in the American League.

COTTON

As the season swung into June, Cotton Nash was called up to Indianapolis of the AAA Pacific Coast League. He was the Esox leading hitter at the time. Nash was a basketball legend at the University of Kentucky. A lanky forward, Nash led Adolph Rupp's early 1960s teams to number one in the national polls. Cotton Nash appeared on the cover of *Sports Illustrated* in December 1962.

Nash also pitched and played outfield for the University of Kentucky, performing so well he was considered a baseball prospect in the $60,000 bonus range. Twelve days after the 1964 NBA draft, Nash signed to play baseball in the Los Angeles Angels organization for a much lesser bonus. The Angels removed a standard clause about competing in another sport.

Cotton Nash preparing to bat in a game at Charlotte. *Author's collection.*

The Lakers, likewise, had no objections and signed him to a multiyear contract. He tried both.

Nash joined the Chicago White Sox organization on May 6, 1967, in a trade sending Moose Skowron to the Angels for Nash and cash. The Sox sent him to Evansville. After a quick start (.310 BA in 17 games), Nash was called up to AAA Indianapolis. Nash hit one home run in cavernous Bosse Field.

BORREGO

The Esox struggled without Nash. They ended the season with just 45 home runs, of which 12 were hit at home. They were the victims of two no-hitters (by Birmingham's Mike Olivo and George Lazerique) and ended with an anemic .226 team batting average. The Esox needed help to contend, and it arrived after the All-Star Game in the person of Rogelio "Borrego" Alvarez, recently released by Knoxville, where he had led the league in home runs the previous season.

Noga called Chicago White Sox farm director Glenn Miller after a positive discussion with Alvarez. "Can he help you?" asked Miller. "Heck yes," replied Noga. "Then sign him," said Miller. The man who teammates called "Borrego" ["lamb" in Spanish] carried a big stick and a sad story of what might have been when he got stuck in Cuba before the 1965 season. He had been named starting first baseman for the Washington Senators over the winter, but his detention while visiting Cuba in the off-season caused him to miss spring training; his major-league shot was gone.

The Esox won four of six road games after the All-Star Game, with Alvarez hitting home runs in three of them. In the first game back home, Alvarez doubled in a run and singled as the Esox retook first place by a half game over Montgomery. Alvarez ended the season tied for the league lead with 19 home runs.

The Best Year

The Rawlings Sporting Goods Silver Glove was awarded to center fielder Angel Bravo, recognizing him as the best fielder at that position in the minor leagues. Bravo also led the Southern circuit in stolen bases with 24. The Venezuela fly-chaser had brief major-league appearances with the White Sox, Reds and Padres from 1969 to 1971, spending the entire 1970 season with Cincinnati. There he became the only Esox player to appear in a World Series game.

A 5–4 win over Montgomery brought lefty Danny Murphy's record to 10-2 and clinched third place for the Sox on the final Saturday home game of the season. The next day, Indiana State University graduate Danny Lazar pitched ten innings in a heartbreaking 2–1 loss that left him short of winning the league's ERA title in the closing game. Lazar's 2.34 ERA was just shy of Birmingham's George Lazerique, who came in at 2.29. Season attendance came to 53,505. Tom Fleming assured followers that his streak of not losing money was still intact. Fleming said the Sox would be back in Evansville in 1968 "if there is a league to play in," as Macon joined Knoxville on the junk heap.

Jesse Queen called it quits after batting .202 in 122 games. The man who had toiled twelve years in the minors went home to join the Elizabeth, New Jersey recreation department in the city where he starred as a high school athlete. Esox manager George Noga's value to the White

Ray Cordeiro, Dick Littleton and Angel Bravo at the 1967 picture day. *Author's collection.*

Sox organization was rewarded with a plum scouting position in southern California. The managerial position was filled by Stan Wasiak, a forty-eight-year-old with extensive experience as both a manager and a player in the minor leagues.

Southern League powerhouse Birmingham dominated the rekindled Dixie Series, winning the seven-game fall classic four games to two over the Texas League champion Albuquerque Dodgers. Reggie Jackson had only 2 hits in 23 at bats for the A's. Catcher Dave Duncan banged out 3 home runs for manager John McNamara's club. The series drew nearly 15,000 in six games split between the two cities. Sam Smith cleaned up the team problem during the annual league meetings in October. Asheville was accepted by owners, and its city council unanimously approved a three-year contract with the Cincinnati Reds in November. Knoxville Smokies owner Joe Buzas said he negotiated a working agreement with the Washington Senators and would move his franchise to Savannah, Georgia.

Walter Dilbeck's brief silence was broken in September. Dilbeck and Associates hired Esox business manager Ray Fletcher to manage a Southern League team he wanted to put in Louisville. Dilbeck made a $65,000 bid for the AAA Toronto Maple Leafs of the International League and acquired Rock Hill (South Carolina), a Cleveland Class-A affiliate in the Western Carolina League. Dilbeck said he had "no plans" to revive the Global League, because expansion was coming.

The Summer of Discontent

Americans were weary of Vietnam. Protests escalated. National elections were coming. Getting butts in Bosse Field seats would be difficult in the coming season. A Bosse Field exhibition game between Chicago's Cubs and White Sox was canceled due to cold and wet conditions. A crowd of over 3,500 was expected. The headlines of the day put the disappointment in perspective. The night before, Reverend Martin Luther King Jr. had been assassinated in Memphis.

Tom Fleming was home readying for the club's home opener while the Esox opened in Savannah. After spending time in his office on the morning of April 19, the Esox general manager complained that he wasn't feeling well. He was taken to Welborn Baptist Hospital just before lunchtime. The fifty-nine-year-old Fleming had suffered a heart attack and was placed in the cardiac care unit, listed in "fair" condition.

The Esox opened at home on April 24, when snow was reported in some northern Indiana cities. New first baseman John Matias blasted a 415-foot home run in a 10–1 Esox route of Charlotte. Only 574 fans braved the cold. The Hawaiian-born Matias was a prospect acquired from the Baltimore organization in a deal that sent Luis Aparicio to the White Sox. Ossie Blanco was another who came in an off-season trade. Ossie split time among first, third and outfield. His .289 batting average was the best of those who played the entire year. Blanco had two stints in the majors, with Chicago and Cleveland.

Future major-leaguers sprinkled the Esox lineup throughout the summer. Cotton Nash was back and split the season between Hawaii

(AAA) and Evansville. Adrian Garrett hit 7 home runs in forty-two late-season games. He spent parts of eight seasons in the majors with Atlanta, the Chicago Cubs, Oakland and California. He crossed the ocean to play for Hiroshima in the Japanese Pacific Coast League for three seasons. Outfielder Ron Lolich, cousin of soon-to-be 1968 World Series pitching hero Mickey Lolich, began the year with the Esox and ended it in Lynchburg. Lolich made appearances with the White Sox and Cleveland Indians from 1971 to 1973.

Gail Hopkins was an All-American catcher for Pepperdine University in 1963 and signed with the White Sox in 1965. He quit baseball after two years and took a job teaching at Pepperdine and was named head baseball coach. His wife was pregnant with their first child. After a year as a head coach, and a father, the baseball bug hit him again. He returned to the White Sox system in the spring of '68. The Sox sent him to AAA Hawaii. After hitting .324 in 22 games there, Hopkins was sent to Evansville, where he duplicated the .324 average in forty-four games for the Esox.

Former Esox star Buddy Bradford made news in the big leagues on July 5 when the Chicago White Sox started the franchise's first "all-Negro" outfield against the Washington Senators just over twenty-one years after Jackie Robinson's Dodger debut. Center fielder Bradford was flanked by Tommy Davis in left and Leon Wagner in right.

BYE-BYE ESOX

The '68 Esox were not good. Manager Wasiak didn't make it through the season in Evansville. On August 1, the White Sox organization sent Wasiak to manage Class-A Appleton and brought Gary Johnson back to Evansville in a rare skipper swap. The demoted Wasiak managed continuously in the minor leagues through 1986, amassing 2,530 victories. That surpassed Evansville's favorite, Bob Coleman, as the winningest manager in minor-league history.

Montgomery swept three straight in July. The third game of the homestand was played in front of a paltry 163 patrons, while most of the city's baseball fans watched the Phillies and Cardinals play on TV. Montgomery's three wins were part of a record sixteen straight Southern League victories. Despite the win streak, Montgomery could not overtake powerful pennant-winning Birmingham.

The futility ended on Labor Day with a day-night doubleheader against Birmingham at home. Just 320 struggled to the Garvin Park venue for the finale. The Esox split the twin bill for their fifty-fifth win of the season. The team's eighty-four losses were the most in Evansville history since the formation of the NAPBL in 1902. Sox attendance was only a little over 35,000. Tom Fleming, whose health problems lingered, hinted that he might not return to baseball the next year.

Weak attempts were made to save the franchise. On October 1, Mayor McDonald was in St. Louis for the annual meeting of minor-league farm directors. His mission was to find a working agreement with a major-league club, a stipulation a group of local businessmen required before they would purchase the franchise. Nothing was offered. The businessmen retreated.

Early November brought hope when local businessman Elmo Henson Jr. said he would attempt to buy the franchise if Bosse Field dressing rooms were remodeled, advertising would be allowed on outfield fences and field conditions were improved. His partner was former Evansville Brave Pete Whisenant. Mayor McDonald informed Chicago White Sox officials he was not interested in providing the city with player personnel like last year. Nonetheless, the mayor was complimentary of the relationship with the White Sox.

Whisenant and Henson met with Columbus, Georgia city officials a week earlier to talk about moving the franchise there. Fleming offered everything for $10,000. That included offices, playing equipment and four sets of uniforms. On December 3, the franchise moved to Columbus, but Henson and Whisenant were not the owners. Fleming said the pair never made a hard and fast offer, so he sold it to another party.

Who bought the franchise? Who else but Walter Dilbeck? By the middle of 1969, the Columbus franchise was in shambles. Dilbeck never delivered the much-need financial support he promised. He spent it elsewhere.

GLOBAL RETURNS

Walter Dilbeck's aim when he acquired Louisville was to convince National League president Warren Giles that the city should be part of the 1969 major-league expansion. In May, he made an application to Giles to consider Louisville as one of two teams added to the National League. The Louisville Colonels drew well at the box office early in the season, making

Dilbeck's application for major-league status seem feasible. Dilbeck planned to plead his case at July's major-league All-Star Game in Houston, but Giles announced that San Diego and Montreal were chosen before he could.

Dilbeck had a contingency plan. Milwaukee attorney Sidney Eisenberg mailed a letter to baseball commissioner William Eckert asking him to authorize the formation of a third major league. Eisenberg was a partner of Dilbeck's in the effort to make baseball a global sport. Dilbeck's All-Star Game visit was used as "sort of an organizational meeting." Dilbeck explained his next play to the *Press*. "We haven't gotten any reply from the commissioner yet, and we hope we don't get one," said Dilbeck. He cited the rejection of Milwaukee and Dallas as expansion teams as the reason new life had been pumped into the Global League idea. Besides the two jilted expansion hopefuls, Dilbeck added that Jersey City, Mexico City, Buffalo and New Orleans were interested and had money, resources and ballparks.

Commissioner Eckert responded in a July letter to Eisenberg. He quoted a major-league rule that laid out the requirements for an application of a new major league. "The executive council will consider your fully-documented application at the appropriate meeting," continued the letter. Eckert wrote that if the application was approved it would be presented to the next meeting of the major leagues for consideration and action. Eckert didn't say no.

Potential Global League member Milwaukee quickly got cold feet. Milwaukee had hosted nine Chicago White Sox games in 1968 that drew almost half of the total attendance for the Windy City South Siders' eight-one-game "home" schedule. That kept Milwaukee on the A-list of future major-league teams. There was talk that the White Sox might move there. A July meeting of potential Global League members in Louisville was postponed indefinitely. Most attributed the postponement to Milwaukee's shift away from the new league.

Dilbeck kept moving the ball forward. He told *Press* sports editor Al Dunning that the league would "definitely" play a limited schedule in 1969. Dilbeck had just returned from three days of talks on the West Coast and said he had four teams from Japan, along with Mexico City, Louisville, Jersey City and Dallas. His Louisville International League franchise would remain intact. The Global League franchise would play there when they were out of town.

Then Dilbeck told the *Courier* that he had "TV wheel" Jack Corbett involved with four Japanese teams. Corbett promised that the league would get 50 percent of Japanese television rights and 100 percent in the United States. Corbett had patented the Hollywood Base, baseball's official base, in 1938. He sued major-league baseball twice. He went all the way to the Supreme Court in 1953, claiming antitrust violations by Commissioner Happy Chandler that prohibited signing Mexican League players for his El Paso minor-league team. He sued Commissioner Frick in the 1960s, claiming he was being blackballed from baseball. He lost both suits.

Dilbeck said the four Japanese teams were solid, because they already had players. To obtain players for the other teams, Dilbeck talked of a tryout camp in Florida to take place in February 1969. Dilbeck said he would offer player contracts comparable to those in major leagues and would share 50 percent of the television money.

A League Is Born

Dilbeck dispatched Rockville general manager Jack White to Japan in September. Accompanying White was Dilbeck's wife, Dorothy. White met with the Japanese baseball commission, who blessed the four Japanese teams in the venture. Walter joined White and his wife in Japan and said the league would "definitely" open in 1969 with eight teams at spring training in Mexico City.

At a September 25 news conference in Louisville, Dilbeck formally announced the formation of his league. Both United Press International and the Associated Press attended and sent stories to nearly every newspaper in the United States. The "loop" was headquartered in Evansville on the top floor of the Ramada Inn on the corner of Sixth and Walnut Streets. Four weeks after the Ramada Inn news release, Dilbeck held another press conference in Louisville to introduce A.B. "Happy" Chandler as league commissioner. Chandler was twice the governor of Kentucky, a former U.S. senator and the man who permitted Jackie Robinson to play in the major leagues as baseball commissioner in 1947.

Chandler accepted the position at a salary of $4,000 per month. The seventy-year-old one-time Evansville resident expressed optimism for the future of the Global League. Excellent organization and financing were his reasons to believe. The press conference ended with Dilbeck noting that only three Japanese teams would play in 1969. He named George Yoshinaga as a vice-president. Yoshinaga was editor of Los Angeles's Japanese American newspaper, *Kashu*, and a former actor and sports promoter. He and Japanese interests would own 25 percent of the league. Having a "colorful halftime show" for thirty minutes after the fifth inning of every game was the first promotional idea.

BIG NAMES

Earlier in 1968, Happy Chandler was under consideration to be Alabama governor George Wallace's vice-presidential running mate in the Democratic primaries. On October 28, with the presidential election looming, Global League commissioner Chandler was posing for pictures with Arnold Edward Davis, the first man to sign a player contract with the league. Davis was employed by the city of Evansville.

Davis, a right-handed pitcher, was born in Chicago and raised in Owensboro. He had no professional experience. He had recently played semipro ball for the Evansville Tigers of southern Indiana's Double-I League. The Tigers were once members of Dilbeck's Stan Musial League. Dilbeck promised to attract good talent to the league by offering $600-a-month salaries, 20 percent of league profits and 50 percent of television revenue, the latter two to be shared among the players. Davis received an undisclosed bonus for signing. Dilbeck revealed his next strategy. "We're going for names," he told the *Courier*, "and old 'Happy' knows them all." Dilbeck wasn't talking about name players. He'd made a gentleman's promise not to raid the major or minor leagues.

One name emerged while negotiating a spring training site lease. Diamond City Park was a six-diamond complex in Daytona Beach that had fallen into disrepair. It was built in 1946 and had reached eyesore status. Four of the fields had no outfield fence, and the other two were fenced with chicken wire. But it was the only Florida location that could handle the 150 players Dilbeck and Chandler planned on for spring training. The league's attorney negotiated a $5,000 one-year lease for the fields from late February to June, with an option for three additional years. The negotiating attorney's life filled a book. *The Man Who Seduced Hollywood: The Life and Loves of Greg Bautzer* was written by James Gladstone in 2014. Attorney Greg Bautzer's clients included Howard Hughes, Ingrid Bergman, Ginger Rogers, Bob Hope and Walter Dilbeck, to name a few.

"I'm interested. I'm very interested," were the words of Baseball Hall of Fame member Johnny Mize when asked about managing a Global

League team. The baseball world knew Mize, and Dilbeck hired him. Two-time minor-league executive of the year Hillman Lyons was brought in as a vice-president at an annual salary of $40,000. At the time of Hillman's appointment, Dilbeck said the league lineup consisted of Louisville, Mobile, Tampa, Jersey City, Tokyo, Ngoya, Osaka and Yokahama. Dilbeck reported that he was negotiating with former Dodger catcher Roy Campanella to manage Jersey City. Toru Mori, a five-time All-Star first baseman in the Nippon Professional Baseball League, was hired by George Yoshinaga to manage his Tokyo Giants. Mori had recently retired from the playing field.

Dilbeck continued at breakneck speed in November. He declared that the Global League would have a 32-man board of directors made up of "16 baseball greats" and 16 bankers to oversee players and finances. Dilbeck claimed that part of the problem was that the baseball players of this era were not in shape. His contracts stated that players "must be in excellent physical condition." If they violated that regulation, they would "forfeit benefits"

Global League founder
Walter Dilbeck Jr.
Author's collection.

The league, said Dilbeck, was negotiating with an attorney representing Howard Hughes, who had recently taken over Sports Network Inc. John Beck was a former Hollywood producer and production executive at RKO Studios representing the Global League. Beck approached the renamed Hughes Sports Network with a proposed TV deal, royalties from which would pay players to the tune of $30,000 per year. Beck said that the league would not raid the minor leagues. Television highlights would include a World Series, to be played in Louisville the first season and move to Japan in season two.

Beck wanted to make a movie of Dilbeck's life and war heroics called *OK, Private Dilbeck*. Beck had produced such notable films as *Harvey* starring Jimmy Stewart and *The Singing Nun* starring Debbie Reynolds. The actor Ryan O'Neal's father, Charles, wrote the screenplay, titled *The Private War of Walter Dilbeck*. It is now in the University of Iowa Library's Special Collections. Years later, Beck introduced Dilbeck to former vice-president Spiro Agnew, and for a brief time they became business associates in the 1970s.

New Rules and Organization

Dilbeck wanted games to be fast-paced, exciting and different. Free substitution would be allowed. The rules permitted pitchers to stay in the game after being pinch-hit for. This pinch-hitting rule applied to any position. A good gloveman might play an entire game without going to bat. A lousy fielder might never put on a glove. Pinch runners could replace slow runners and return later to pinch-run again while the replaced runner stayed in the game. Intentional walks would send runners to first base simply by informing the umpire, a practice that has since been adopted in the major leagues.

More names emerged at the Ramada Inn organizational meeting. Danny Menendez, a twenty-two-year veteran of major-league baseball, was named vice president of player procurement. Princeton, Indiana native Jack White was tabbed vice-president and general manager. Former vice-president of Atlanta's International League teams, Dick King, returned to baseball after a three-year hiatus to fill another VP spot.

Now organized, Dilbeck announced spring training would begin March 1 at the Diamond City fields and rolled out more names. Training would be run by Mize and Enos Slaughter, another well-known baseball name.

Former Houston Astros pitching coach Gordon Jones would assist during training. Dilbeck said that he expected Campanella and ex-Boston pitcher Mel Parnell to join them at Daytona Beach. The final bit of news was a new lineup of clubs. The six-team league now had two each from the U.S. (Jersey City and New Orleans), Japan (Tokyo and Yokahama) and Latin America (San Juan, Puerto Rico, and Caracas, Venezuela).

Global Domination Always Sounds Good

Al Dunning, sports editor of Evansville's evening *Press*, described the hustle and bustle surrounding the opening of the Global League world headquarters at the Ramada Inn in January. A truckload of phones pulled up to the "nerve center" of the new major league. Men hauled beds out of rooms and moved in desks. A secretary told Dunning that ex-major-leaguer John Blanchard was on the phone looking for a job. Hillman Lyons rattled off names like Don Larsen, Norm Siebern, Johnny Romano and Rocky Colavito and claimed that more than two thousand aspiring players would come to training camp.

Dunning caught up with Dilbeck. "Fact is, one of the biggest names in show business is arranging an hour's time for our opening game," touted Dilbeck, "and the way it looks, we'll open on TV on Sunday, April 6, probably in Dodger Stadium in Los Angeles." Dilbeck did not divulge this big name. There would be no home teams in the Global League. Teams planned to visit minor- and major-league parks for fifty exhibition and ninety regular-season contests. Dunning likened it to a "floating crap game."

Stu Miller, a sixteen-year veteran of big-league pitching, signed as a player-coach. Former Evansville Hub Al Todd joined as a coach in early February. Todd had played for Bob Coleman in 1929 and 1930 and toiled eleven years as a major-league catcher. Al's son Hank, a southpaw pitcher from Ithaca College in New York, signed a player contract. Bill McKinley joined as supervisor of umpiring. McKinley spent twenty years as a major-league umpire and was looking to get back into the game.

A *Sporting News* advertisement announced two-day tryout camps "for the exciting new Global League" in five cities during the last two weeks of February. The ad encouraged free agents with AAA or major-league experience to contact the league at its 600 Walnut Street headquarters. Long Beach, California, Bryan, Texas, along with Mobile, Baton Rouge and

BASEBALL LEAGUE TRYOUT CAMPS
for the exciting New
GLOBAL LEAGUE
to be held in the following cities:

HOUGHTON PARK — LONG BEACH, CALIF. . . . . . FEB. 19th-20th
TRAVIS PARK — BRYAN, TEX. . . . . FEB. 21st-22nd
HARTWELL FIELD — MOBILE, ALA. . . . . FEB. 23rd-24th
CITY BASEBALL PARK, BATON ROUGE, LA. . . . . . . FEB. 25th-26th
SAM W. WOLFSON PARK—JACKSONVILLE, FLA. . . FEB. 27th-28th

All Sessions Commence at 10 a. m.

Camps will be under personal supervision of Gordon Jones, former pitcher with Giants, Cardinals, Orioles and pitching coach of Houston Astros. Assisted by Stu Miller.

GORDON JONES   JOHNNY MIZE   ENOS SLAUGHTER   STU MILLER

ATTENTION: All Free Agents with previous experience in AAA or Major Leagues. Contact Global Baseball League, 600 Walnut Street, Evansville, Indiana 47708

★ THE SPORTING NEWS, FEBRUARY 8, 1969 ★

Global League headquarters were located on the top floor of Evansville's Ramada Inn. *Courtesy of the* Sporting News.

Jacksonville would host the camps under the supervision of Gordon Jones. Photos of Jones, Mize, Slaughter and Miller adorned the ad.

Dilbeck claimed that some ten thousand tryout applications were received and that around two hundred major-league players had written inquiries. Numbers from the camps in California and Texas were difficult to obtain, but at other sites, Dilbeck's claims weren't even close. Fifteen hopefuls showed up in Mobile, resulting in three contracts. Baton Rouge and Jacksonville had twelve and twenty-three attendees, respectively, with only six signees.

Chandler and Dilbeck approached officials of the Hughes Sports Network. Their lofty goal was to secure a $6 million television contract. Rumors of financial difficulties were circulating, and many were saying the venture would never get off the ground without a television deal. Hughes officials turned down the pair's offer.

Newspapers reported that Global League offers were made to Don Drysdale, Jim Bunning, Bill Mazeroski, Roberto Clemente, Brooks Robinson, Juan Marichal, Joel Horlen, Jim Maloney, Ron Santo and Jim Fregosi. The players were allegedly offered four-year contracts at $150,000 per year and 2.5 percent equity shares in the league. Some players were intrigued, given there were few $100,000 yearly contracts in the big leagues at the time. Hank Aaron revealed that he received a two-year, $500,000 offer and turned it down.

A week into March, Hillman Lyons said he was getting ready to open spring training on March 17, and they were still negotiating a TV contract. He said the Global League had a "no raid" agreement with the major leagues, meaning they wouldn't go after its players. Everything Lyons stated seemed incongruous with other stories of the day.

Spring training opened in mid-March. The Tokyo team arrived at Diamond City Park on April 1. Over one hundred players reported with contracts. Former major-league star Chico Carrasquel was introduced as manager of a team representing his home country of Venezuela. Former New York Giants pitcher Ruben Gomez took the reins of the San Juan team from his native Puerto Rico. Retired major-league pitcher Ed Rakow was on site as a player-coach. Mize and Slaughter ran the show on the fields. The Venezuela Oilers edged the Alabama Wildcats, 3–2, in the first official training game. Besides the two exhibition game opponents, the Jersey City Titans, San Juan Suns, Tokyo Dragons and Dominican Republic Sharks rounded out the league.

Jimmy Mann of the *Tampa Bay Times* was one of the few sportswriters in the country to comprehensively cover spring training. Mann wrote a three-part series titled "The Global League Story," detailing the quirkiness of the venture. He shed light on the "almost" television deal. The deal, wrote Mann, depended on the league's ability to attract current major-league stars. When none of the ten or more players bit on Dilbeck's offers, Hughes Sports Network backed off of a more realistic $3 million deal.

Mann mused about players, coaches and Dilbeck's money. He wrote that Dilbeck arrived at spring training with $100,000 in cash on him. He bought $14,000 in airline tickets for Opening Day game destinations and gave $16,000 to the Tokyo team for its troubles getting to the United States. He paid for players' Daytona Beach hotel rooms and gave each $15 a week for "walking around money." Player backgrounds varied. Some had no professional experience. Those who had played organized ball were mostly recently cut from mid- to low minor-league teams.

The camp's success was measured by the fact that most teams left with a full roster of players. Players, coaches and team officials used their Dilbeck-provided one-way tickets to the Dominican Republic, Puerto Rico and Venezuela for Opening Day games. The flights left without Los Angeles manager Stu Miller. Miller left his post to go into the insurance business and planned to open a liquor store in San Carlos, California.

Of his Global League experience Miller later said, "I was conned."

GAMES AND GONERS

On Thursday, April 24, 1969, the Global League accomplished something critics believed would never happen. It played a real game. Behind the four-hit pitching of former minor-leaguer Juan Quintana, Venezuela defeated Japan, 6–0, in Caracas. U.S. press coverage of the opener amounted to a one-paragraph AP filler story. Global League scores rarely made the scoreboard section of sports pages after that.

Coverage was worse in the Dominican Republic and Puerto Rico. Crowds were generally just a few hundred per game. League officials decided to move all games to Venezuela, where the league was gaining interest. The problem in Venezuela was that gate receipts didn't match the turnouts. Managers of the government-owned ballfields controlled the take.

A game in Valencia drew five thousand. When Mize and Slaughter went to get their cut, they were told, "Sorry, you didn't make any money." The two were told the game netted $80 after expenses and that those proceeds were given to the Venezuelan team. Dilbeck told Al Dunning about a Caracas crowd of twenty-one thousand. "We ought to have a gate of $20,000 if we let the Venezuelans steal everything in the ballpark," said Dilbeck. "But they told us we owed them $500 just to get out of the stadium." A Caracas hotel stopped serving food for three teams and threatened to evict eighty-eight players unless a $12,000 bill was paid. Nearly $90,000 was owed to Caracas hotels. Contacted, Dilbeck said he sent $80,000, but it was "held up" by formalities at local banks.

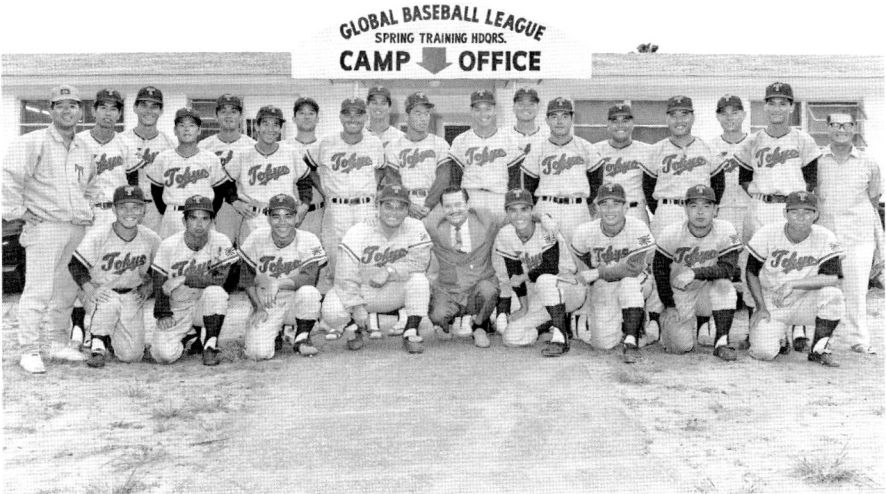

The Tokyo Dragons at Global League spring training with Walter Dilbeck. *Author's collection.*

Money troubles mounted, and Commissioner Chandler quietly disappeared from the scene. Chandler claimed he was a "forgotten man" with no duties. He said he had never been paid but fortunately spent none of his own money on the venture. Next to go was player procurement official Danny Menendez. He took a job with the Montreal Expos, saying, "The Global League is a fiasco." Menendez was disgusted with the ethics of the league. Of the March attempt to raid major-league players, he said, "I didn't want to destroy the structure of baseball. I didn't want to be part of something that wasn't right." Menendez wasn't paid any of his $35,000 annual salary. "You can't squeeze blood from a turnip," quipped Menendez.

The Venezuelan dream was over on June 1. The Puerto Rico team was the first team to leave, without incident. The remaining five teams said they were heading back to the United States. League spokesman Paul May maintained that they would pick up playing games wherever they could in the United States after regrouping in Columbus, Georgia. The league was charged with violating Venezuelan immigration laws by allowing its players to work in Caracas using "tourist cards." Some players sold their belongings and bought airfare home.

Dilbeck showed up in Caracas with $55,000 in cash in a cardboard box. He gave Johnny Mize and Enos Slaughter $1,500 each and $1,000 each to some of the remaining players. Most players and coaches found their way back to the United States. The Tokyo team was boarded and ready to leave after their plane fare was paid by check. The check bounced. They were evicted from their flight. Their paychecks and a $20,000 check to the Hotel El Conde also bounced. In early July, a local judge ordered them not to leave the country. All twenty-five players were moved to one hotel room and could leave only for meals at the Japanese embassy.

BAPTISTS TO THE RESCUE, SORT OF

The league was collapsing around him when Dilbeck pulled a rabbit out of his hat. On June 17, Dilbeck confirmed the sale of the Global League to the Baptist Foundation of America for $4.1 million in foundation notes. The purchase included Dilbeck's Lake-Reel-Em-In, a 110-acre piece of prime real estate in western Kentucky, for $1.1 million. "I spent one million for the Global League and sold it for three million," boasted Dilbeck. The Baptist Foundation was headquartered in Los Angeles. Its president was Reverend Dr. Thomas Sherron Jackson, who said he liked the league's strict training rules. Dilbeck struck the deal on January 12 in East St. Louis, Missouri, but kept it quiet until now.

Dilbeck remained league president and announced that all six teams would gather in Columbus, Georgia, and continue playing. The Japanese team was still in Venezuela, along with fourteen league officials. Dilbeck said he was unable to help, because they now worked for the Baptist Foundation. It wasn't until the first week of August that arrangements were made for the Japanese team to leave. On August 11, the Dragons took off for Evansville and arrived the next day. George Yoshinaga said he personally put up over $3,500, and Dilbeck kicked in $1,000, to fly the team out of Venezuela. "Why did I ever get involved," said Yoshinaga of the debacle, adding that he "should have had his head examined." His players lost an average of fifteen pounds in Venezuela. Yoshinaga said the Venezuelans treated the Dragons "worse than dogs."

The Dragons got back to the business of playing Global League baseball. The league obtained permission to practice at Lafayette Park in nearby Princeton, Indiana. Dilbeck booked an August game between the New York Titans and the Dragons at the two-thousand-seat Joe Hargis Field in in Rockport, Indiana. Dilbeck and Baptist Foundation president Jackson watched as the Tokyo Dragons pummel New York, 20–4. The teams paused after the fifth inning for a wedding ceremony between Dragon pitcher Hieda Koya and Elsa Molina, a woman Koya met while stranded in Venezuela. Dr. Jackson presided. "We'll definitely play next year, with eight teams too," proclaimed Dilbeck after the game.

Their next game was at Fort Campbell, Kentucky, a venue near the Baptist Foundation's recent acquisition, Lake-Reel-Em-In. After a few more games around Evansville, the teams dispersed, and the league moved from the playing field to courtrooms to squabble over unpaid bills. The grand experiment was over.

The Happy Ending

Evansville was the hub of one of the grandest experiments and failures in organized baseball history. While Dilbeck's Rome burned to the ground, Evansville mayor Frank McDonald quietly laid the groundwork for something big.

McDonald revealed that International League president George Sisler approached him in April asking if the city would "take" Louisville in his AAA circuit. Owner Walter Dilbeck wasn't making rent payments on the Louisville Fairgrounds stadium and was far behind on other payments. The league wanted Evansville to assume the franchise. The season was four days away. McDonald knew it was a recipe for disaster. Luckily, Louisville shopping mall magnate William Gardner, a nephew of Boston Red Sox owner Tom Yawkey, stepped in and paid $80,000 in delinquent Dilbeck obligations. Dilbeck was stripped of his AAA club. Evansville was spared almost certain failure. McDonald understood that the baseball world was still interested. He made it clear that going forward he was not interested in anything below Class-AAA.

In September, Evansville lost another chance for a AAA club when the International League chose Wichita to fill an open spot. McDonald was still confident. He had been told that Evansville was one of twenty-four cities deemed most desirable for Class-AAA. The next possibility was the revitalized American Association League. Indianapolis spokesman Max Schumacher was in favor. "I'd like to see Evansville in our league," said Schumacher. "It might be a good rivalry for us."

In November, American Association president Allie Reynolds announced that his league would expand to eight teams. "Evansville is under consideration," Reynolds told the Associated Press. At 130,000 residents, it would be the smallest city in Class-AAA. Reynolds said "if" Evansville was selected, it would be affiliated with the Montreal Expos. Montreal was out of the picture when Reynolds visited Evansville to meet with McDonald. Accompanying Reynolds was Minnesota Twins farm director Sherry Robertson. Days later, Evansville was offered a team. The Twins presented Evansville a player development contract for the 1970 season. The club would be owned by Adam K. Grafe, a graduate of Terre Haute Wiley High School and Rose Polytechnical Institute. Grafe owned a successful engineering firm in Dallas and was a longtime friend of McDonald.

The Twins asked the city to add more lights and that the field be in playing condition. "We'd also like to sell beer," stated Robertson. The perennial "uh-oh" was in the mix. The school corporation still controlled concessions. A week went by. And another. On the last day of November, Sherry Robertson told reporters that they were working out the details of the field lease. "I anticipate no problems," said Mayor McDonald. The final lease terms needed to be approved by the school board, and beer appeared to be the only thing left to be concerned about.

The *Courier* broke the news on December 4 with the headline "AA Confirms Evansville In." The school board approved the sale of beer in Bosse Field for professional baseball games. A few minutes after the vote McDonald confirmed that the Minnesota Twins' AAA franchise belonged to Evansville.

"This is the finest brand of baseball the City of Evansville can ever hope to attain," beamed McDonald. Mayor McDonald was right. Evansville was at the Mount Everest of minor-league baseball. The mayor and new owner achieved what no one else in the town's history had: brews and baseball. *Courier* sports editor Bill Fluty called it "a giant step out of the Dark Ages."

One imagines that city officials celebrated over a bottle of beer.

7

EPILOGUE

GLOBAL DISASTER AND AAA TRIUMPH: 1970 AND BEYOND

On the first Sunday of the new decade, Communist China gave up trying to gain a seat in the United Nations. "Instead," announced Chairman Mao Tse-Tung, "China will work to obtain a franchise in the Global Baseball League." The revelation was contained in the *Sunday Courier and Press* section "Side Look at News."

Walter Dilbeck and his Global League offices were evicted from the sixth floor of the Evansville Ramada Inn shortly after Mao Tse-Tung's announcement. Baptist Foundation notes were practically worthless. Dilbeck tried to sell them at a discounted price, with no takers, so he traded $3 million of notes back to the BFA for 147,000 shares of Standard Computer and Pictures unregistered stock, valued at $10 per share. "I figured that $1.5 million in stock is much better than $3 million in BFA notes," said Dilbeck. It turned out that both Standard and parent Computrealty were under investigation by the Securities and Exchange Commission. The stock was practically worthless.

Then there was the strange case of Reverend Sherron Jackson. In September, the *Wall Street Journal* reported that the BFA was under investigation by the California attorney general, the SEC, the IRS, the U.S. Post Office and the Department of Justice for issuing countless millions of promissory notes in exchange for property and services. By December, a federal judge enjoined Jackson from selling BFA assets and was named receiver of all BFA assets. The assets were virtually worthless. "When the BFA deal was made they showed me papers that showed $28 million in assets," said Dilbeck. Dilbeck was not alone in being duped. One financial statement falsely showed $386 million in assets.

In 1973, the Baptist Foundation of America was put out of business. At the time, it had $26 million in liabilities and $15,000 in assets. A year later, Reverend Jackson was sentenced to eighteen months in prison for conspiracy to defraud and mail fraud. Jackson was busted again in 1976 for conspiracy, making false statements, mail fraud and interstate use of money obtained by racketeering. The reverend was shown to have had ties to Los Cosa Nostra and faced twenty years in prison.

The Global League disaster was the beginning of the end for the Dilbeck empire, although he continued to wheel and deal years after it failed. He met former vice-president Spiro Agnew in 1974 and signed him as a consulting partner, hoping Agnew could help attract Arab investors to a proposed lakeside resort development in western Kentucky. Agnew ended the partnership after a year, accusing Dilbeck of "a calculated scheme to promote your image at the expense of my integrity."

In 1976, Dilbeck pleaded guilty to filing false tax returns in 1969 and spent sixty days in the Vanderburgh County Jail. When released, he was a changed man. As a born-again Christian, he spent the last fifteen years of his life "happier than he had ever been in his life," according to his wife, Dorothy. In 1984, he filed for personal bankruptcy with $1.31 million in personal debt, mostly from the baseball debacle. Walter Dilbeck Jr. died in 1991. His greatest disappointment was the failure of the Global League. Dilbeck loved baseball and Evansville. There was nothing to suggest his efforts were anything but sincere. He was simply out of his league.

The year 1970 witnessed the remarkable resurgence of minor-league baseball. The Evansville Triplets deal went smoothly compared to the chaos of the Global League. Carolyn Traylor's entry was chosen from the 3,218 who entered the team naming contest. Hers was one of 73 submitting the winning name. A panel of local sportswriters broke the tie by voting on the best twenty-five-word description of his or her choice. Traylor won a $500 savings certificate with a poem.

Triplets it should be,
Here are my reasons THREE:
The team is A times THREE,
In the Tri-State they'll be,
Twins parent have TRIPLETS, agree?

On March 31, 1970, the Vanderburgh County Alcoholic Beverage Commission officially approved and sent a permit to the state board allowing beer to be sold at fifty-seven Triplets games, excluding those played on Sundays. The triplet sons of Ralph and Mary Lou Huff were chosen as the official Triplet bat boys. Triplet brothers Dan, Doug and Don were on the field when the club began the first of fifteen years representing Evansville in the American Association, during which they never dipped below the 100,000 mark in yearly attendance and won the 1975 Little World Series of AAA. The Triplets drew over 1.7 million fans before the franchise was purchased and moved to Nashville in 1985. The peak at the gate was in 1972 and set an Evansville record of 147,807.

Longtime sports broadcaster Marv Bates called home games behind the WGBF microphone. For road games, Bates re-created the action in real time from the Evansville studios with the help of newsman Fred Rollison, who gleaned play-by-play reports from a Western Union teletype machine and ran them to Bates. Bates interspersed sounds from two tape recorders to simulate thirty-two different crowd and background

The 1970 Evansville Triplets. *Courtesy of University of Southern Indiana.*

Extras file into Bosse Field for the 1991 filming of *A League of Their Own*. Evansville Courier & Press.

noises. "We're not trying to fool the fans," said Bates. "Just want to give them the best possible show."

The limelight shined on Bosse Field in the summer of 1991, when Hollywood came to town for the filming of the motion picture *A League of Their Own*, starring Lori Petty, Rosie O'Donnell, Madonna, Geena Davis and Tom Hanks. The ballpark served as the home field of the Racine Belles in the film. The real Belles appeared in Bosse Field for a charity game after World War II. All-American Girls Professional Baseball League game footage and the league's World Series were shot there under the direction of Penny Marshall.

Professional baseball returned in 1995. The Evansville Otters of the independent Frontier League are the most successful franchise in that league's history. The Otters were the first to hit 1 million in attendance, in 2005. In 2013, they surpassed the 2 million mark. That season, a record single-game crowd of 8,253 filled Bosse Field. The franchise is still thriving under the ownership of local attorney Bill Bussing.

Only Fenway Park and Wrigley Field surpass the ballpark's longevity. If you love baseball, visit Bosse Field and take in an Otter game.

BIBLIOGRAPHY

Books

Adelson, Bruce. *Brushing Back Jim Crow: The Integration of Minor-League Baseball in the American South*. Charlottesville: University Press of Virginia, 2007.

Auker, Eldon, and Tom Keegan. *Sleeper Cars and Flannel Uniforms*. Chicago: Triumph Books, 2001.

Bjarkman, Peter C. *Baseball with a Latin Beat: A History of the Latin American Game*. Jefferson, NC: McFarland, 1994.

Blahnik, Judith, and Phillip S. Schulz. *Mudhens and Mavericks*. New York: Penguin Books, 1995.

Cava, Pete. *Indiana-Born Major League Baseball Players: A Biographical Dictionary, 1871–2014*. Jefferson, NC: McFarland, 2015.

Chadwick, Bruce. *Baseball's Hometown Teams: The Story of the Minor Leagues*. New York: Abbeyville Press, 1994.

Clark, Dick, and Larry Lester, eds. *The Negro Leagues Book: A Monumental Work from the Negro Leagues Committee of the Society for American Baseball Research (SABR)*. Cleveland, OH: Society for American Baseball Research, 1994.

Eaton, Ron. *Local Legends: The Stories Behind the Headlines: 100 Years of Southwestern Indiana Sports History*. Evansville, IN: M.T. Publishing, 2008.

Freedman, Lew. *African American Pioneers of Baseball: A Biographical Encyclopedia*. Wesport, CT: Greenwood, 2007.

Gladstone, James. *The Man Who Seduced Hollywood: The Life and Loves of Greg Bautzer, Tinseltown's Most Powerful Lawyer*. Chicago: Chicago Review Press, 2014.

Gorman, Robert M. *Death at the Ballpark: A Comprehensive Study of Game-Related Fatalities, 1862–2007.* Jefferson, NC: McFarland, 2008.

James, Bill. *The New Bill James Historical Baseball Abstract: Revised Edition.* New York: Free Press, 2003.

Johnson, Lloyd, ed. *The Minor League Register: Compiled from the Society for American Baseball Research's Minor League Stars, I, II, III, and Original Research.* Durham, NC: Baseball America, 1994.

Johnson, Lloyd, and Miles Wolff, eds. *The Encyclopedia of Minor League Baseball: The Official Record of Minor League Baseball.* Durham, NC: Baseball America, 1993.

Lee, Bill. *The Baseball Necrology: The Post-Baseball Lives and Deaths of More Than 7,600 Major League Players and Others.* Jefferson, NC: McFarland, 2009.

McCarter, Mark. *Never a Bad Game: Fifty Years of the Southern League, 1964–2014.* Middleton, WI: Lineup Books/August Publications, 2014.

McConnell, Bob, ed. *Going for the Fences: The Minor League Home Run Record Book.* Phoenix, AZ: SABR, 2009.

National Association of Professional Baseball Leagues. *The Story of Minor League Baseball, 1901–1952: A History of the Game of Professional Baseball in the United States with Particular Reference to Its Growth and Development in the Smaller Cities and Towns of the Nation—The Minor Leagues.* Columbus, OH: Stoneman Press, 1952.

O'Neal, Bill. *The Southern League: Baseball in Dixie—1885–1994.* Austin, TX: Eakins Press, 1994.

Pietrusza, David. *Major Leagues: The Formation, Sometimes Absorption and Mostly Inevitable Demise of 18 Professional Baseball Organizations, 1871 to Present.* Jefferson, NC: McFarland, 1991.

———. *Minor Miracles: The Legend and Lure of Minor League Baseball.* South Bend, IN: Diamond Communications, 1995.

Plott, William J. *The Negro Southern League: A Baseball History, 1920–1951.* Jefferson, NC: McFarland, 2015.

Riley, James A. *The Biographical Encyclopedia of the Negro Baseball Leagues.* New York: Carroll & Graf, 1994.

Smith, Allen, and Ira Smith. *Low and Inside: A Book of Baseball Anecdotes, Oddities, and Curiosities.* New York: Doubleday, 1949.

Society for American Baseball Research. *Minor League Baseball Stars.* Vol. 1. Manhattan, KS. Ag Press, 1978.

———. *Minor League Baseball Stars.* Vol. 2. Manhattan, KS: Ag Press, 1985.

———. *Minor League Baseball Stars.* Vol. 3. Birmingham, AL: EBSCO Media, 1992.

Sullivan, Dean A. *Early Innings: A Documentary History of Baseball, 1825–1908*. Lincoln: University of Nebraska Press, 1995.

———. *Late Innings: A Documentary History of Baseball, 1945–1972*. Lincoln, NE: Bison Books, 2002.

Sullivan, Neil J. *The Minors: The Struggles and the Triumph of Baseball's Poor Relation from 1876 to the Present*. New York: St. Martin's Press, 1990.

Newspapers

Evansville Argus
Evansville Courier
Evansville Courier & Journal
Evansville Courier & Press
Evansville Journal
Evansville Journal News
Evansville Press

Periodicals

Baseball Digest
Sporting Life
Sporting News
Sports Illustrated

Guides

Baseball Almanac
Reach's Guide, 1885–1930
Spalding Guide

Other References

Baseballinwartime.com
Baseball-reference.com (used for all minor-league statistics)
Browning Genealogy. www.browning.evpl.org

Center for Negro League Baseball Research. www.cnlbr.org
Evansville-Vanderburgh Public Library
Historicevansville.com
Hoosier State Chronicles. Operated by the Indiana State Library. Indiana's
    Digital Historic Newspaper Program
Jewishbaseballmuseum.com
Local History Database: Evansville, Indiana. www.local.evpl.org
Negrosouthernleaguemuseumresearchcenter.org
SABR Biography Project
Vanderburghcohistoricalsociety.com
Willard Library, Evansville, Indiana

INDEX

ABOUT THE AUTHOR

*K*evin Wirthwein grew up in Evansville, where he attended Harrison High School. He studied journalism at Butler University in Indianapolis and wrote and edited for the *Butler Collegian* newspaper and the *Drift* yearbook. After graduation, Kevin was a sportswriter and sports editor for the *Brownsburg Guide* newspaper in Brownsburg, Indiana. There, he won a Hoosier State Press Association Award for his weekly sports column. He was a staff writer for *Trap & Field Magazine* and served briefly as editor of the *Zionsville Times* in Zionsville, Indiana, before returning to Butler to earn an MBA degree and enter the business world. He is a member of the Society for American Baseball Research and the Vanderburgh County Historical Society. Kevin is married and has four lovely daughters.

Visit us at
www.historypress.com